WE WILL CARRY ON

By
Judy & Trena Rogers

xulon
PRESS

Copyright © 2009 by Judy & Trena Rogers

We Will Carry On
by Judy & Trena Rogers

Printed in the United States of America

ISBN 978-1-60791-665-9

All rights reserved solely by the authors. The authors guarantee all contents are original and do not infringe upon the legal rights of any other person or work. No part of this book may be reproduced in any form without the permission of the authors. The views expressed in this book are not necessarily those of the publisher.

Unless otherwise indicated, Bible quotations are taken from The New International Version (NIV), Copyright © 1973,1978,1984 by International Bible Society; Message Bible (MSG), Copyright © 2002 by Eugene H. Peterson; and New Living Translation (NLT), Copyright © 1996,2004 by Tyndale House.

www.xulonpress.com

We dedicate this book to our husbands, Bob and John, for your continued love and support; Rob, for writing music that glorifies God, and to our families who have encouraged us to "carry on."

Publish His glorious acts throughout the earth. Tell everyone about the amazing things He does. Psalm 96:3

Contents

FOREWORD	8
The Solid Rock	10
New Beginnings	12
Called to Sing	14
New Car or New Album?	16
Never Doubt a Miracle	18
Putting Off Falsehoods	19
A Captive Audience	20
A Star is Born	22
Long Hair	25
The Best of the Best	26
Finger Lickin' Good?	28
A Senior Moment	30
More Tuna Fish Anyone?	32
Welcome to Dollywood	33
Christmas Elves	36
Obeying the Holy Spirit	38
Faith, the Size of a Cruise Ship	40
Perseverance	42
It's a Mission Trip, Not a Cruise	44
Angels on Guard	46
Mannish Water	48
A Prophecy Fulfilled	50
Feast for Six	51
A Gift from God	52
Empty Nest	54
Take Me Out To The Ballgame	56

The Perfect Family	58
A Common Bond	60
End of the Road	62
Headed to the Races	66
"Many Rules" Motel	68
Walking on Water	70
Smile Awhile	72
The Experience of a Lifetime	74
No Hands! No Hands!	76
Dressing Room Dilemmas	78
Trials and Travelations (Part 1)	80
Trials and Travelations (Part 2)	82
Spur-of-the-Moment	84
Angel Dog	86
Defining our Roles	88
We Will Carry On	91
Memories	95
Holiday Food	106
God Is Great	108
We've Come To Worship You	110
Wonderful To Me	111
You're the One Who is Holding My Heart	112
In The Name of Jesus	113
Closer To You	114
Welcome to the Family of God	115
I Can Do All Things Through Jesus	116
A Living Sacrifice	117
What people are saying about Judy and Trena Rogers	119
ACKNOWLEDGEMENTS	123

FOREWORD

A tragic accident occurred; a little girl not quite five years old was being pulled out of the water and given mouth-to-mouth resuscitation. The mother, in a panic-stricken state of shock, suddenly realized that because of her own backslidden condition, she had never told the little girl about Jesus.

The man who had been working on her looked up and said, "I'm sorry, I cannot get her to breathe." Her frail little body had already turned grayish in color. The mother fell to her knees and cried out to God, "Please, God, let my little girl live so I can tell her about you."

About that time, the ambulance drivers came. The look on their faces told her she had lost her little girl. In desperation, she cried out louder, "Lord, please let her live so I can tell her about you." A huge crowd had formed, and ordinarily the mother would be too embarrassed to say she had ever given her life to Jesus; but the crowd didn't seem to bother her now, and she continued to cry out to the Lord.

The ambulance drivers, who had seen many drowning cases, just shook their heads and said, "We're sorry, she's gone." Then a miracle took place. God breathed the very life back into the little girl. The ambulance quickly took her to the hospital. The mother listened to the doctor as he sadly told her, "She's still unconscious and in a coma. We'll have to keep her and watch her carefully, as there could be brain damage."

The mother went into the hospital room and knelt by the little girl's bed. She talked to God again and said, "Even if she lives and there is brain damage, she won't understand when I tell her about Jesus." Then God opened the eyes of the little girl and she said, "Mommy, why are you crying?"

Well, that mother never stopped telling the little girl about Jesus, and today, that little girl is all grown up and is now telling others about Jesus.

I thank God that I'm able to tell you this story. I'm the mother, and Trena is that little girl. With the music ministry God gave us many years later, we have shared the good news of Jesus Christ all over the world through our music and testimonies. Maybe you need a miracle in your life. Our God is a God of miracles!

The Solid Rock

As a result of the miracle that Mom had seen God do, her life was changed forever. She and I began attending Sunday School and church service, but Daddy stayed home. Although he was very grateful for the preservation of my life, Daddy still was not ready to re-commit his life fully to Christ. He had accepted Christ as his Savior when he was a young man, but due to a lack of discipleship in his life, Daddy stopped going to church.

One Saturday, a couple of years after the drowning incident, our family pulled off the road so Daddy could fish for a while. As soon as he came to a stop, he realized that he had driven into soft sand, and we were stuck. To add to his frustration, Mom and I serenaded Daddy with the hymn "On Christ the Solid Rock I Stand; all other ground is sinking sand." Finally, Daddy walked to the nearest gas station for help while Mom and I stayed with the car. While waiting for the tow truck driver, Daddy went to get a drink from the water fountain inside the station. As he looked up, there on the wall was a life-size picture of Jesus. Daddy's heart began to soften at that moment.

The next morning, we were in church as a family. As we stood to sing the first hymn, Daddy just shook his head and Mom and I smiled as the music minister announced the song, "The Solid Rock I Stand." Daddy re-dedicated his life to Christ at the time of invitation. God is a God of miracles!

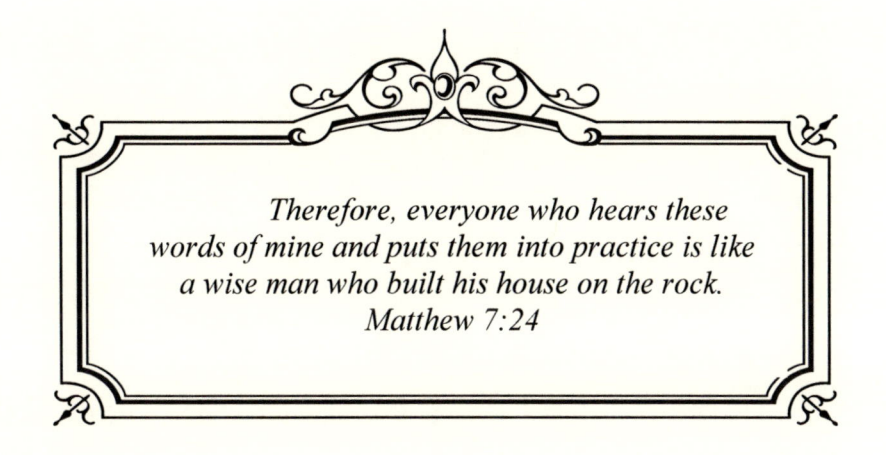

*Therefore, everyone who hears these
words of mine and puts them into practice is like
a wise man who built his house on the rock.*
Matthew 7:24

We Will Carry On

New Beginnings

Mom and I loved to sing together around the house or in the car. So, when our music minister asked us to sing a duet in church, we were very excited. However, when the time came for us to sing, we were very nervous. We were so scared, that during the whole song, Mom's legs were shaking and I could not keep my upper lip from quivering. Our first thought was, "Well, nobody will ever ask us to sing again."

Right after the service, a lady from another church came up to us to ask if we could sing a few songs at her church for a Mother/Daughter banquet. We were shocked. God still wanted to use us in spite of our weaknesses. We graciously said we would sing for the banquet, and thus began a music ministry.

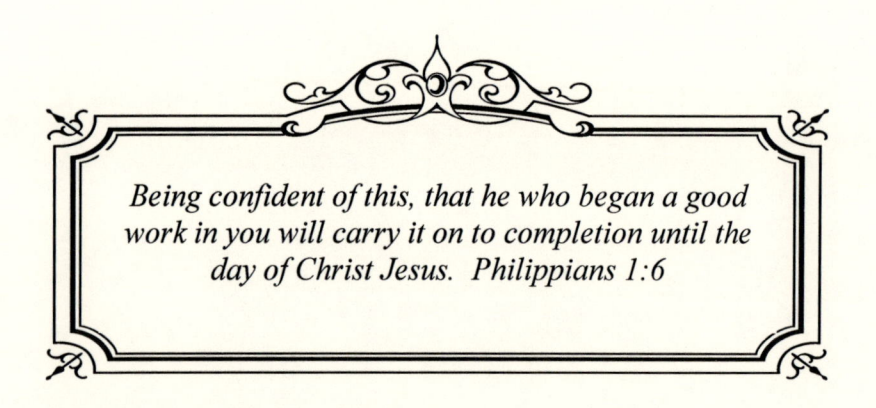

Being confident of this, that he who began a good work in you will carry it on to completion until the day of Christ Jesus. Philippians 1:6

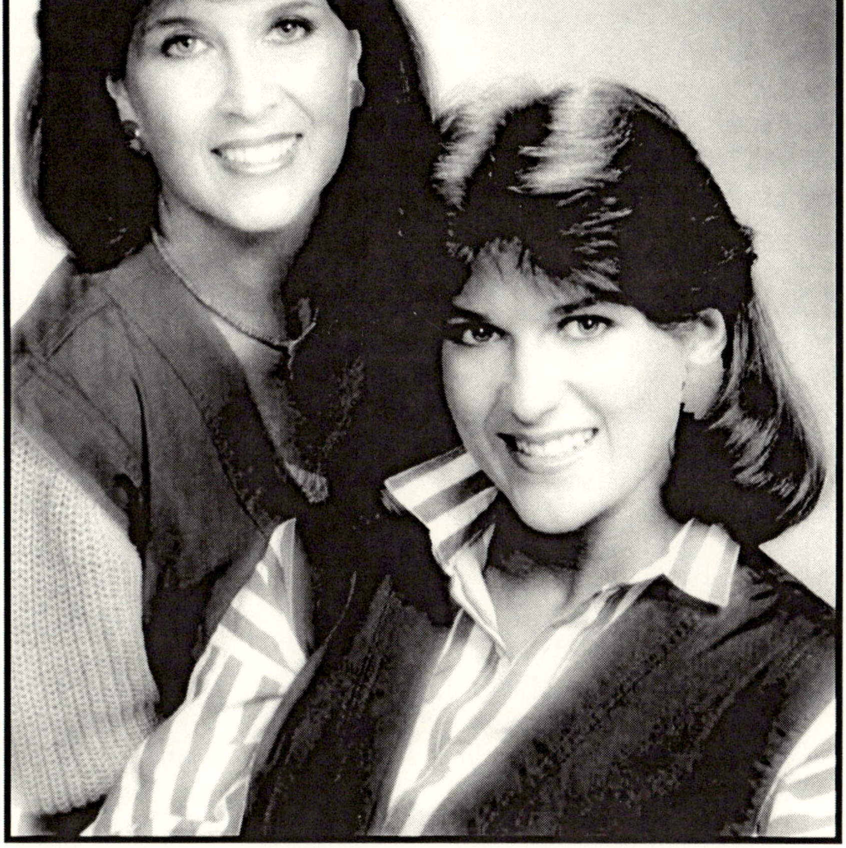

Called to Sing

In our first year of ministry, people began asking if we had any albums for sale. Not only had we never recorded an album, but we had never even thought about it. I could not understand why anyone would ever want to buy a recording of Judy and Trena Rogers. My own feelings of inadequacy made me feel like I could never be one of those top named Christian artists.

I remember the wise words of my Godly mother, "Trena, we have a story to tell concerning how God has delivered our family, and how He can do the same for others. If our testimonies and our music are the tools He chooses to use, then who are we to question His methods?" I never questioned my calling again.

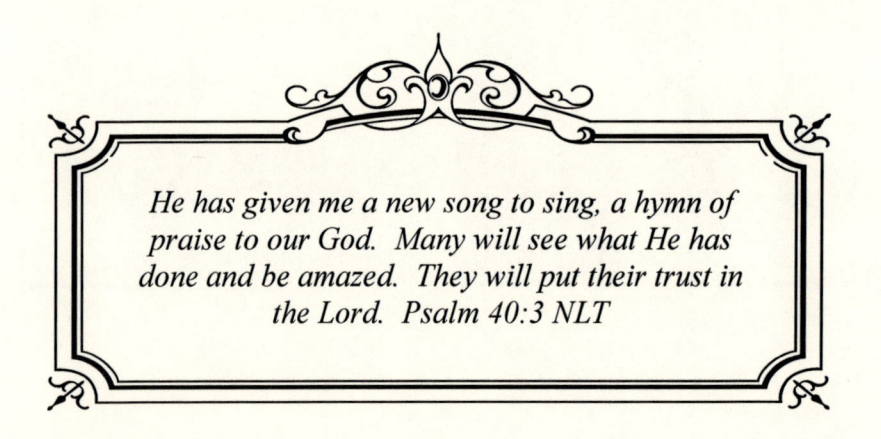

> *He has given me a new song to sing, a hymn of praise to our God. Many will see what He has done and be amazed. They will put their trust in the Lord. Psalm 40:3 NLT*

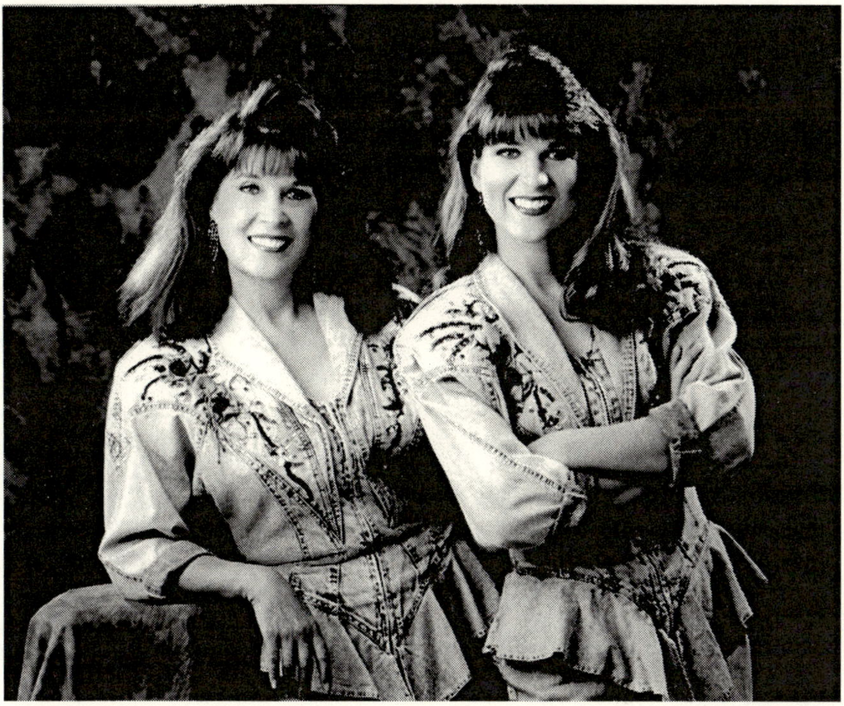

We Will Carry On

New Car or New Album?

Mom and I were not sure how we were going to pay for our first album, but that didn't stop Mom. She knew it would take a lot of money, we did not have, to record.

Mom's car was an old Ford Pinto wagon. It had a lot of miles on it, and it needed to be replaced. She and Daddy had been saving money for months so that Mom could have a new car.

Through much prayer and sacrifice, Mom decided to drive the old Pinto a little longer so that we could use the money she and Daddy had saved to pay for the album.

A record company, Windchime Records, invited us to record with them. Our first album was called "Friends." Years later, we have our own record label and have recorded over 10 albums.

Eventually, we traded in that old car for a ministry van. God is faithful to provide!

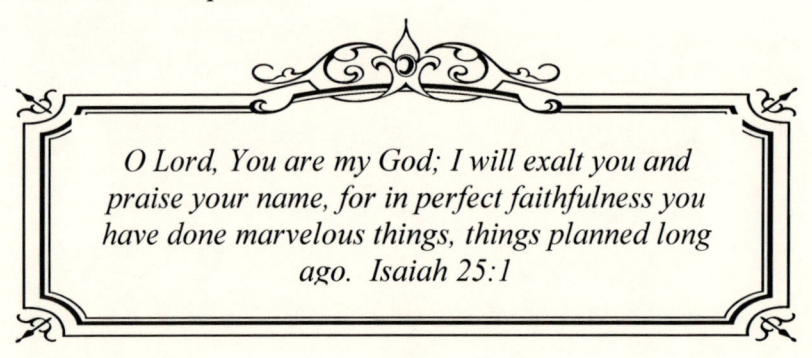

> *O Lord, You are my God; I will exalt you and praise your name, for in perfect faithfulness you have done marvelous things, things planned long ago. Isaiah 25:1*

Our First Ministry Van

Never Doubt a Miracle

For several months, we prepared for the recording of our first record project. The recording studio in Nashville was booked, and a sizable deposit was already sent. Three weeks prior to our recording date, I contracted a bad virus. Mom took me to the doctor, but the medicine he prescribed did not help. My symptoms only worsened. Three days prior to leaving for Nashville, my throat was badly inflamed, and I was heavily congested. Mom called our producer, fully expecting to have to cancel, losing our deposit money. However, in faith, he encouraged us to come anyway so we could start the recording process with the instrumentalists and the background vocalists.

I slept for most of the drive from Florida to Tennessee, coughing all the way, which is disastrous for a vocalist. In spite of the fact that I had no voice to even speak, we decided to start recording some vocal tracks our last night there. Our Christian producer grabbed our hands to pray, believing God to supernaturally intervene during our recording session. In faith, Mom and I stepped up to the microphone to start recording. For the next seven hours, I never coughed or needed a tissue. God's presence allowed me to sing better than I had ever sung before. Everyone in the studio witnessed a miracle of God. Our family will never doubt that God is still working miracles today.

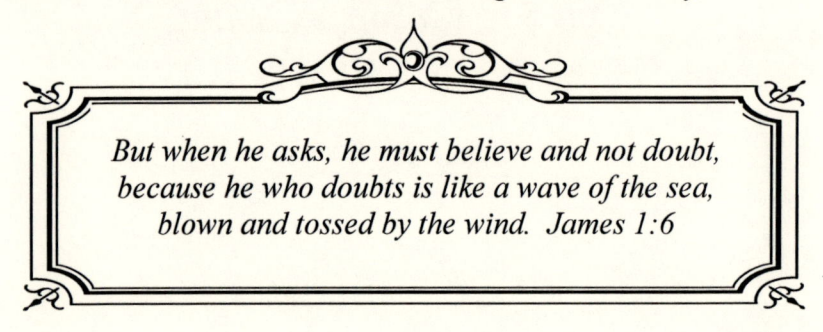

> *But when he asks, he must believe and not doubt, because he who doubts is like a wave of the sea, blown and tossed by the wind. James 1:6*

Putting Off Falsehoods

We were very excited about our evening performance at a Christian television station in Greensville, North Carolina. We were scheduled to sing two songs during a live 30-minute program. This called for some very special preparations.

The long standing joke in our family was, "It's better to look good than to feel good." Since the TV cameras would be focusing in on our hands holding the microphones, Mom and I decided to get manicures for just this occasion. However, instead of letting a professional do the job, we decided to do it ourselves. We went to the store, looked at our options, and chose the cheapest fake nails along with the cheapest nail glue.

That evening, Mom and I sang our first song without any problems. We were quite proud of ourselves. We sounded good, and we looked good, especially our fingernails. It wasn't until about midway through our next song that God humbled us. I was singing the second verse when a false nail literally popped off one of my fingers on my right hand and landed about three feet in front of me. Trying to keep our composure, Mom and I kept singing. Within seconds, another nail flew off my right hand. I had to finish the song holding the microphone with my left hand, and I hid my right hand behind my back. I was sure all of Greensville had witnessed the catastrophe!

Mom and I could no longer contain ourselves when the producer thanked us for coming and said in all seriousness, "You ladies have the prettiest hands and nails."

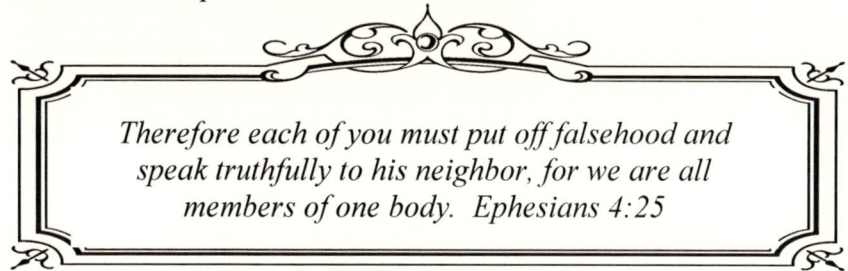

Therefore each of you must put off falsehood and speak truthfully to his neighbor, for we are all members of one body. Ephesians 4:25

A Captive Audience

Pastor Steve, a very encouraging friend in the early years of our ministry, would always welcome us to his church any time we were traveling near his area in Georgia. On one occasion, he asked if we would be interested in singing in a prison. We agreed to go not knowing what to expect, but trusting God to work His plans through us. This particular prison held teenage boys to 25-year-old men. They were some of the worst criminals in Georgia. Most of the prisoners would never be released from prison, and those that were released would likely return for future offenses. Most of the men had nowhere to go after their release, which led them right back into a life of crime.

Pastor Steve informed us on the way to the prison that the living conditions were unlike many prisons. Because the prisoners knew they would likely never live outside of the prison, many would try to commit suicide. Therefore, items like light bulbs were not allowed in their cells as they might try to hurt themselves. Even Christian materials held together with staples were considered dangerous to the prisoner.

We performed for a full room of young men who were just glad to get out of their cells. At the end of our concert, we asked if there was anyone who would like to commit their life to Christ. Several raised their hand, but were not allowed to leave their seat to come forward for prayer. So, we led them in a prayer of repentance and commitment as they remained seated. We were very excited when we saw the number of men who had prayed. However, our excitement didn't last long. After we left the prison, Pastor Steve informed us that he, along with several other pastors, tried many times in the past to reach these men with the Gospel, but their hearts were so hard that they never made any life changes. We were disappointed, but we committed to pray for the young men.

Almost a year past before we received a call from Pastor Steve. This time, he wasn't calling to book a concert. He was calling with great news. He first explained that he would have called sooner, but he wanted to make sure that the circumstances were legitimate. One of the young men that had raised his hand had sincerely committed his life to Christ that day. He began to read the Bible and live a life of holiness. Miraculously, he was released from prison and began attending seminary to become a pastor.

We remembered the captive audience we had at the prison that day, and we thanked God for setting one captive free!

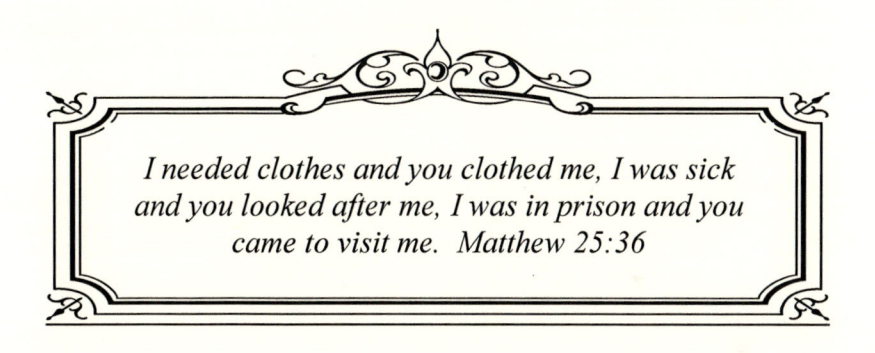

I needed clothes and you clothed me, I was sick and you looked after me, I was in prison and you came to visit me. Matthew 25:36

A Star is Born

As a little girl, Mom always dreamed of being a star and singing on stage. She would always walk around the house singing songs. Her Mom used to tell her that some day her name would be up in lights. We always joked and laughed about this until one day when we were on our way to a concert. Just as we turned onto the road that led to our destination, there was a bank sign that had our name flashing in lights. We immediately pulled off the road so that we could get pictures.

It was not Broadway, but it was better. God heard the prayer of a little girl in Knoxville, Tennessee, and blessed her with the opportunity to sing for Him. Now she's singing the praises of the biggest star ever born, the bright Morning Star!

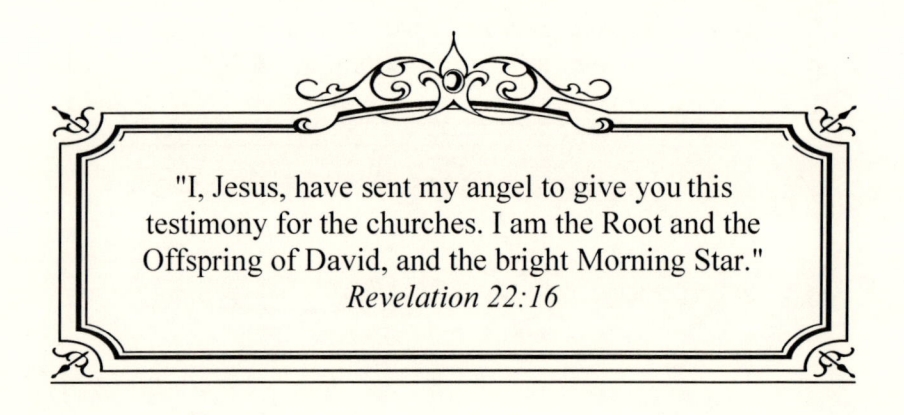

"I, Jesus, have sent my angel to give you this testimony for the churches. I am the Root and the Offspring of David, and the bright Morning Star."
Revelation 22:16

FIRST FEDERAL
LAKE COUNTY
PRESENTS

FIRST FEDERAL
LAKE COUNTY
JUDY & TRENA

We Will Carry On

Long Hair

As we began working on our second recording project, Mom started to take part in the production process, and she wanted only strong Christians involved. For some reason, her perception of a strong, Christian man in the work place was a short haired, well dressed person. Upon arriving in Nashville to our thoroughly searched and prayed over Christian record company, we met our producer, the instrumentalists, and background singers, all people who had worked with some very well known artists. We felt very confident that our prayers had been answered.

We then met our engineer, the person who would have complete control of the sound for the finished project. Much to our surprise, he had very long hair and was dressed in raggedy shorts and an old t-shirt. As we were all leaving the studio that first night, our engineer commented that he was on his way to church and would just have to usher in the clothes he was wearing. The look of shock on Mom's face was priceless!

During the next four days, we got to know this man and see him as someone who took pride in his work, had patience and kindness, and was someone who truly loved the Lord. God taught us to never judge a person by what they wore or how they styled their hair. We are so thankful that God does not look at our outward appearance but instead looks at our heart.

Man looks at the outward appearance, but the Lord looks at the heart. I Samuel 16:7

The Best of the Best

In 1984, Mom decided to enter our ministry into the Sanford Christmas Parade. Our brand new album had a song titled "Jesus is Your Ticket to Heaven" that opened up with a train whistle. We decided that Mom and I would pantomime that song while riding on a decorated float. A friend of ours had a children's life-sized train that we placed on a flatbed trailer decorated with clouds and angels. With the help of several children from our church and a portable sound system, the Christmas float was a huge success. We even won a trophy for "Best Religious Float."

We knew we were going to win, but not because we were the best. We were just the ONLY religious float in the parade!

Our God is also the Best of the Best. Not just because He is, but because He is the One and ONLY God!

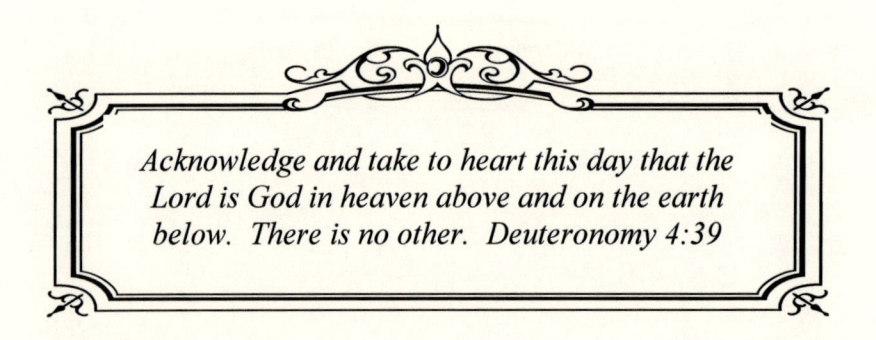

Acknowledge and take to heart this day that the Lord is God in heaven above and on the earth below. There is no other. Deuteronomy 4:39

1st Place Religious Float

Sanford Christmas Parade 1984

Finger Lickin' Good?

Some of our fondest memories are going out to eat after church concerts with pastors or music ministers and their families. The common bond that Christ brings between total strangers always intrigues and amazes us.

Occasionally, we have been invited to share a meal in the home of the host pastor. One time a pastor's wife made spaghetti and meat sauce ahead of time and put it in the slow cooker. By the time everyone sat down to eat, we were served spaghetti mush. Mom, Rob, and I pushed more of our food around the plate than we ate.

We were very excited when our hostess brought out two beautiful pies. Mom and I chose the chocolate cream pie. She served our slices. As she proceeded to ask Rob which slice he would like, the pastor's wife ran her fingers up the knife to remove the chocolate residue and licked her fingers! Although Rob is 6'3" and was obviously very hungry, he politely declined any more food.

As soon as we were back in the van, Rob asked, "Mom, can we please stop at the nearest Taco Bell?"

For the kingdom of God is not a matter of eating and drinking, but of righteousness, peace and joy in the Holy Spirit, because anyone who serves Christ in this way is pleasing to God and approved by men. Romans 14:17-18

A Senior Moment

In looking back over the years, we have met thousands of people during our travels. However, two special ladies stand out in our minds. The first was a sweet, elderly lady who came to our concert on a Sunday evening. She shared with us that she was 101-years old and still very active in her church. That was an encouragement to all of us that God could use us if we were willing, no matter our age.

The other lady was in her eighties and had been a member of her church for a long time. She admitted after our concert, that although she attended church faithfully, she had never asked Jesus to forgive her of her sins and to be the Lord of her life. That night, during a time of commitment, she gave her heart to Christ. This is one reason why, no matter where we perform, we always have an altar call or a time of commitment. From children to senior citizens, everyone needs Jesus.

That if you confess with your mouth, "Jesus is Lord," and believe in your heart that God raised Him from the dead, you will be saved. For it is with your heart that you believe and are justified, and it is with your mouth that you confess and are saved. Romans 10:9-10

We Will Carry On

More Tuna Fish Anyone?

On one particular trip, we stayed with a dear lady who made us some delicious tuna fish sandwiches for lunch. We really enjoyed the conversation around the table. Our hostess kindly offered us seconds at which time we all looked over to see her cat on the kitchen counter eating out of the tuna fish bowl. Our hostess was terribly embarrassed, but we all had a good laugh as we graciously declined a second helping with, "No, thank you."

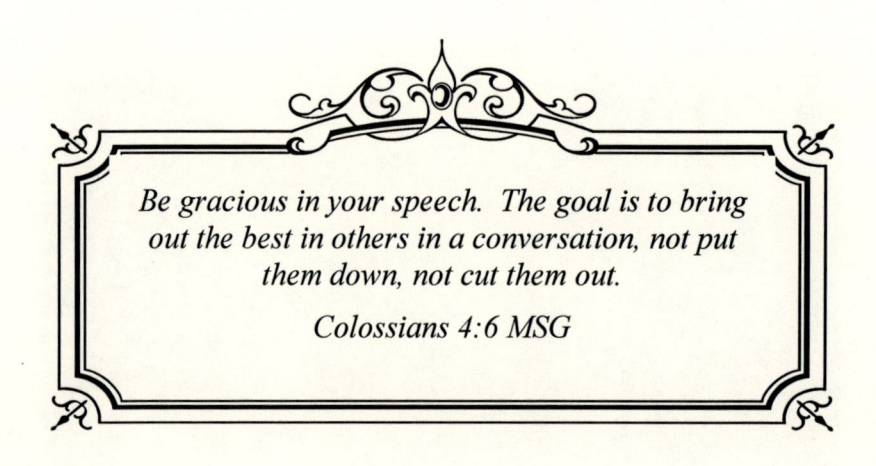

> *Be gracious in your speech. The goal is to bring out the best in others in a conversation, not put them down, not cut them out.*
>
> *Colossians 4:6 MSG*

Welcome to Dollywood

It had been a long 13 hour drive to Nashville. Our only other plan for the day was a dinner meeting with our record producer to discuss our upcoming new album. We arrived at the downtown hotel in jeans and t-shirts. We were tired and disheveled. Usually, Mom and I are very careful to refresh our make-up and hair, but all we cared about was checking into the hotel and taking a nap before dinner.

On our way to the room, we saw a large sign that said, "Dollywood Auditions in Banquet Room." Mom, always thinking positively, says, "Let's check this out." In my normal skepticism, I replied, "Mom, we sing Christian music, and they probably want secular music and dancers." So, I went on to the room while Mom did a little more investigating. As she entered the large banquet room, Mom approached the table where three Dollywood talent scouts were sitting, preparing for the next audition. She inquired about the auditions, and they informed her that these auditions had been booked for three months. She thanked them politely and began to leave. Out of sheer determination, she turned around, handed them a brochure and tape of our music, and told them, "If any audition times become available, we are staying in this hotel for the next four days."

I was already lying in bed about to fall asleep by the time Mom came up to the room. She had not been there five minutes when the phone rang. To our surprise, it was the Dollywood talent scouts. They told us that they had just had a cancelation, and that if we could come down right now, we could audition. Mom and I have never changed clothes or repaired make-up and hair so quickly! I still remember complaining all the way down the elevator, "What are we going to sing? We look awful! Theme parks don't want our style of music." We decided to sing a comedy rendition of "I Shall Not Be Moved." When we finished, they thanked us and said they would contact us if they decided to hire us. We graciously said goodbye, and decided that maybe God just had us there to be a witness to those people that day. Putting the audition behind us, we spent the rest of our time in Nashville working hard on our record project, and then headed home to Florida.

It was about three weeks later when Mom and I received a call from Dollywood. We had been chosen to sing for a gospel event that they present once a year. Our assignment was four sets, 20-minutes each. We were shocked! They continued to invite us for the next twenty-two years, allowing us to share our testimonies and songs. To this day, I am still amazed at how God orchestrated His plan for Mom and me to sing at Dollywood. I never would have thought that Judy and Trena Rogers would be singing for a theme park, but God did!

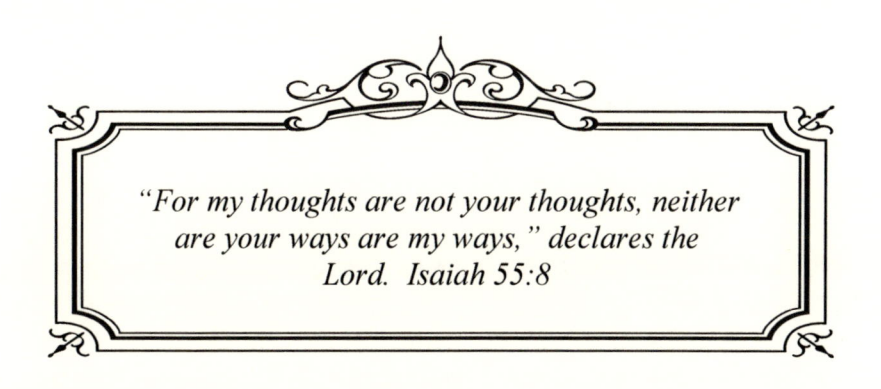

"For my thoughts are not your thoughts, neither are your ways are my ways," declares the Lord. Isaiah 55:8

Christmas Elves

Appropriate attire has always been a priority in our ministry. However, this has not always been an easy task. There have been times when we have looked for months just to find coordinating outfits that are modest and reasonably priced. Our dress code for church concerts has always been very professional, but theme parks, such as Dollywood, required more of a glamorous stage show appearance.

One particular year, Dollywood's entertainment department invited us to sing for their Christmas Season Celebration on one of their main stages. This was quite an honor. Our first assignment: find the perfect outfit for such a great occasion. With our mission in mind, we headed for the mall. We concluded that our costume needed to be primarily red, a color good for the stage. It also needed sequence or beads for the glamorous effect. In only one day, we found the ever popular leggings combined with the long beaded sweater that covers the hips. To finish off that great look, we bought red suede boots.

On the day of our show, we were escorted to a very small room back stage that housed a couple of chairs and a tiny mirror. Without a full length mirror, we had to depend on each other to finish our hair and makeup. It wasn't until we were about to walk out on the stage that we were able to get a good look at ourselves. We both began to laugh. There was nothing we could do to remedy the situation. The announcer was introducing us, and we had to gain our composure so we could perform.

It was hard to concentrate during our show; for every time we looked at each other, we would get the giggles. With our red sweater, red leggings, and red boots, we knew we looked like Santa's elves!

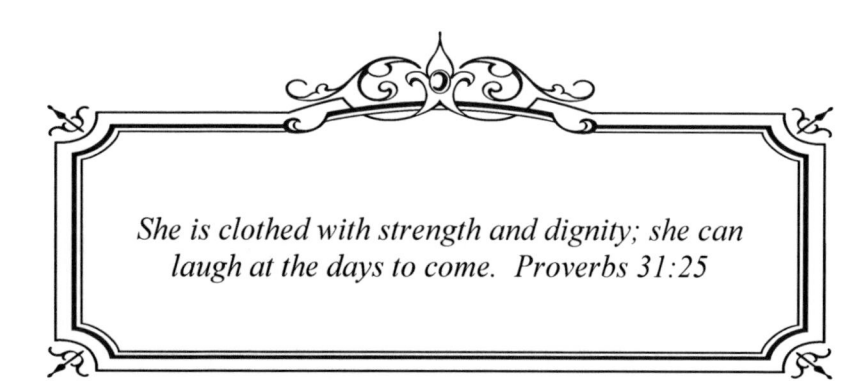

She is clothed with strength and dignity; she can laugh at the days to come. Proverbs 31:25

37

Obeying the Holy Spirit

We were preparing to perform on an outdoor stage at Dollywood Theme Park when the Lord spoke to Mom's heart about what we should sing. We tried to keep each show a little different as some people would come back to listen to a later performance. Several times during the day, Mom had felt we should sing "Shekina," a slow ballad that I sing as Mom interprets through sign language. I didn't want to perform the song because, usually at a theme park you do very lively, up tempo music as it is a fast paced, fun atmosphere. Even after praying, I talked Mom out of performing the song as I was afraid people would walk away. Prior to our final performance, the Spirit of God impressed upon Mom for the third time that we were to sing "Shekina." Not wanting to dishonor my mother, I reluctantly agreed to perform the song.

After the concert, a husband, wife, and their teenage daughter walked up to us and thanked us for the song and the sign language. They proceeded to tell us how they had really enjoyed their day. However, their daughter was deaf and unable to enjoy the singing performances throughout the park. She and her family were elated, as they knew this song was something special just for her. How amazing is our God that He would have her there at just the right performance! How blessed we were because we were obedient to the Holy Spirit!!

Those who live according to the sinful nature have their minds set on what that nature desires; but those who live in accordance with the Spirit have their minds set on what the Spirit desires.
Romans 8:5

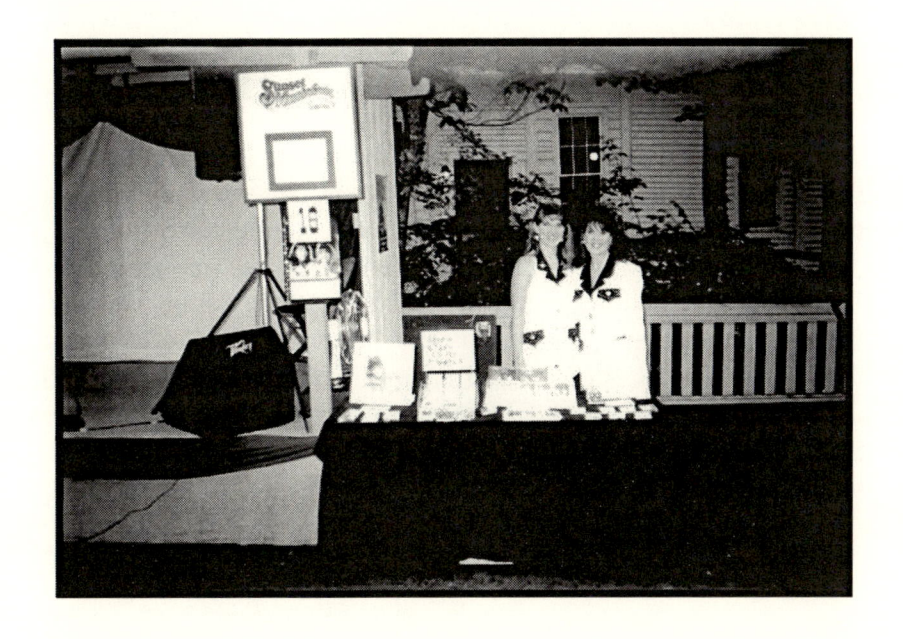

We Will Carry On

Faith, the Size of a Cruise Ship

While driving to a T.V. station to sing for a Christian telethon, Mom was looking through a magazine and spotted an advertisement for a cruise ship. Mom said, "Look at this! Wouldn't you love to go on a cruise someday?" I replied that cruises were very expensive and that I didn't think I would be going on one any time soon. Mom, believing nothing is too big for God, said, "God delights in giving us the desires of our hearts. Maybe we can even perform on a Christian cruise." I laughed out loud and sarcastically said, "Right! Only big name artists get to do that!!" Mom's spirit would not be crushed. She came right back with, "Lord, You've heard our conversation. Your will be done!"

After arriving at the station, we had a sound check and waited our turn to sing for the telethon. While we were waiting, the station manager introduced us to a nice gentleman who was a guest for that evening's events. Before long, we performed our first song and then waited to be called again. While we were waiting, the gentleman we had met earlier came up to us and said, "Have you girls ever performed on a Christian cruise?" We both just looked at each other, grinning, and replied, "No, why do you ask?" That day was the first booking of four Christian cruises we would be blessed to take.

The apostles said to the Lord, "Increase our faith!" He replied, "If you have faith as small as a mustard seed, you can say to this mulberry tree, 'Be uprooted and planted in the sea,' and it will obey you."
Luke 17:5-6

Perseverance

The second time Mom and I sang on a cruise ship, we were also the cruise directors for the organization that hired us to sing. We were responsible for over a hundred people, keeping them on schedule, and making sure everything ran smoothly on a six-night, seven-day cruise to the Caribbean. We were expected to lead an early morning Bible study, direct the shore excursions, perform evening concerts, and finish every night with a midnight devotional. Basically, we were up in the morning at 6:00 a.m. and getting to bed by 1:00 a.m. each night. It was hard work!

To make matters worse, on the sixth day, the ship was returning to Florida in a storm that had twenty-five foot seas. Mom and I both woke up sick to our stomachs. However, Mom was determined to do her job and teach the morning Bible study. So, with me still in bed, she headed for the front of the promenade deck where the large room was located. Almost all of the ship's employees were sick. Mom observed small paper bags placed along the hallway hand rails for people to use in case they couldn't make it to the restroom. When she entered the room, chairs were sliding across the floor with each crash of the waves over the bow of the ship. Five brave people actually showed up for the Bible study. Mom read a five minute devotional, prayed, and headed back to the room.

By lunch time, all the crackers on the ship were eaten, and the waves had subsided to about fifteen feet. Our final group meeting was scheduled for after lunch, which about thirty people actually attended. Mom and I were still very sick. Midway through Mom's "Wouldn't you love to take another cruise?" speech, she turned a lovely shade of pale. She stopped talking, grabbed a small paper bag, turned her back to us, and vomited. She politely wiped her mouth, turned back around, and said, "Now, where was I?" Talk about your perseverance!! Everyone was astonished at Mom's ability to finish a job. She lived out her faithfulness to God, and her integrity on the job. I was really proud of her that day!

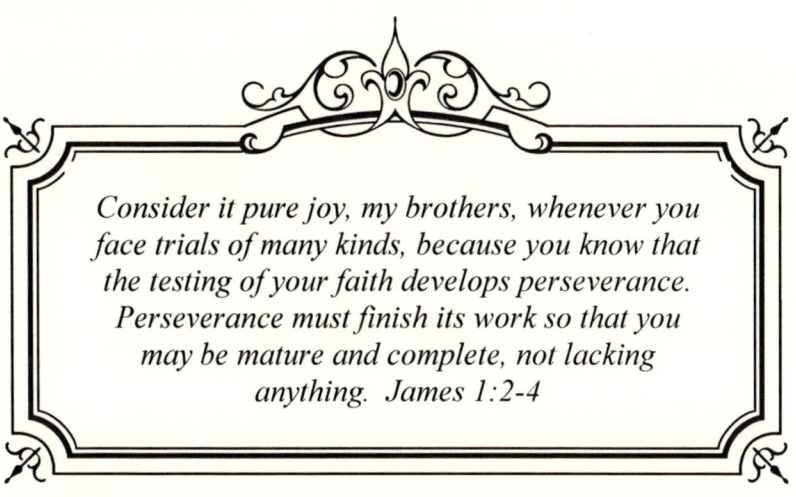

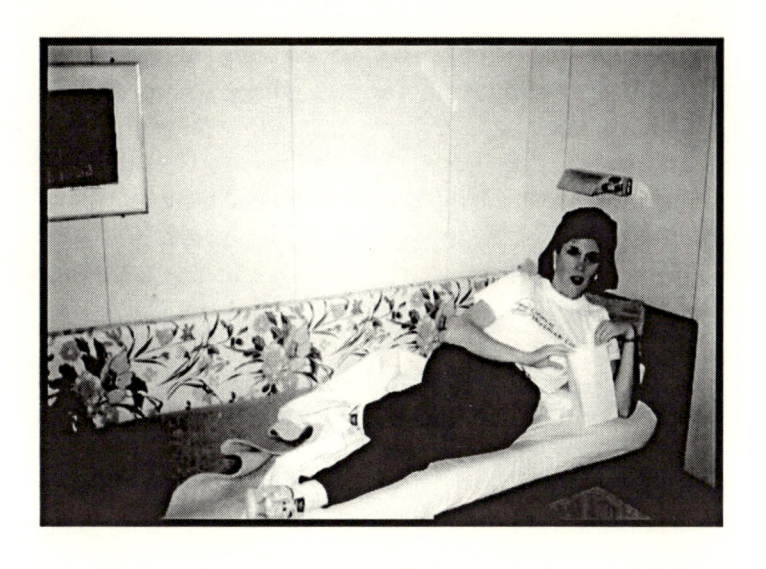

> *Consider it pure joy, my brothers, whenever you face trials of many kinds, because you know that the testing of your faith develops perseverance. Perseverance must finish its work so that you may be mature and complete, not lacking anything. James 1:2-4*

It's a Mission Trip, Not a Cruise

In the earlier years of our ministry, Mom always made sure that we looked our best both on and off the stage. Now, most artists don't really dress up in route to a concert or for airline flights. However, Mom used to tell me, "You never know when we're going to run into a pastor or music minister, and we want to always look our best!"

Our dear friend, Dan Tyler, president of the New International Bible Institute, invited our ministry to go on a mission trip to Jamaica with a group of their student missionaries. We would provide the music for the services. Never having experienced the mission field, we pictured the Jamaica you only see on television commercials. So, Mom made sure we dressed meticulously for the flight. Upon arriving at the airport, we noticed that we were the only women in the group in dress suits and white high heels. Everyone else was wearing comfortable clothing and shoes. Dan greeted us warmly, but I noticed he had a bit of a mischievous smile on his face as he commented how nicely we were dressed. The flight wasn't too long, but by the time we picked up our luggage and started to drive to our destination, we were tired and our feet were sore.

It was only when we pulled up to our lodging that we realized just how overdressed we were. When the van came to a stop in front of an old, small wooden house on stilts, we laughed, thinking Dan was playing a joke on us. "No," he laughingly replied, "you and the rest of the ladies will be here for the next four days." Humbly, we gathered our luggage, and stumbled across the rocks and dirt to get to the front door. By the end of the week, we had to throw our brand new white high heels in the garbage. After all, this was a mission trip, not a cruise!

> *Your beauty should not come from outward adornment, such as braided hair and the wearing of gold jewelry and fine clothes. Instead, it should be that of your inner self, the unfading beauty of a gentle and quiet spirit, which is of great worth in God's sight. I Peter 3:3-4*

We Will Carry On

Angels on Guard

While on a mission trip to Jamaica with mission-aries from the International Bible Institute, we had a scary incident occur. All of the women were housed in one home near the host church, while the men were housed about five miles away in the pastor's home. A sweet elderly lady and her maid welcomed us into her home. Before you picture a large, well decorated mansion, consider six women in a small four bedroom home with one bathroom, no running water except a dripping faucet, no air condition, no electricity, and wood slat floors. During the day, you could see the ground beneath the house through the floor. The "alarm clock" was one very loud rooster that made his presence known at the break of dawn.

On our third day, our mission team took a trip to the marketplace in Montego Bay. Mom and I documented the day with a new video camera. It was obvious that we were tourists.

After the church service that evening, everyone looked forward to a good night's rest. However, around two o'clock in the morning, Susie, our cinematographer, placed her hand over Mom's mouth and told her to wake up quietly. Susie and Jan had come into our room to inform us that someone was outside. The dog was barking, and we could see the light of someone's cigarette in a shrub near the house. I grabbed the only "weapon" we had, a piece of sugar cane. By now, the rest of the women were awake. At the sound of a glass window breaking, we heard the maid yelling something in her native language to the intruder. Everything was quiet after that, including the dog. The maid told us that the intruder was gone, and that she would report it to the police in the morning.

Everyone was back in their beds and trying to go to sleep. Although Mom tried to say it quietly, everyone in the house heard her tell me, "Trena, you sleep for ten minutes, and then I'll sleep for ten minutes. That way, one of us can be awake at all times to be 'on guard.'" Jan and Susie must have heard Mom's outrageous plan because a burst of laughter came from their room. One of the missionaries yelled out, "Well, I've got angels around me, and I'm going to sleep!" At least somebody got a good night's rest.

That morning, the police told us that the maid had identified the man, and that he was a criminal who had just been released from prison. He had followed us from the marketplace, and probably wanted our equipment.

That night, we stayed with the host pastor, his wife, and the rest of the missionaries. It was crowded, but at least there was running water and solid floors. Best of all, there was no rooster!!

For He will command His angels concerning you, to guard you in all your ways.

Psalm 91:11

We Will Carry On

Mannish Water

Our mission trip to Jamaica was an eye opening experience for us. The people were kind and generous. They were especially generous with their food. Our first night there, they served us ackee and boiled green bananas. Ackee is a fruit that can be poisonous if it is not ripened when you eat it. The edible part of the fruit is a yellow color that looks like scrambled eggs when cooked. Your eyes tell you you're eating scrambled eggs, but your taste buds tell you something totally different! The bananas are very starchy and bland tasting. Being careful not to offend our new friends, we politely took a few bites and set aside the rest. Naively, we assumed we would lose a few pounds over the next few days. However, we were pleasantly surprised with servings of delicious foods like roast duck and jerk chicken.

To make the trip a true Jamaican experience, our missionnary group was invited to a wedding that our host pastor was officiating. The young couple encouraged us to enjoy the food and festivities. It was then that Dan, our leader, decided to have a little fun. He brought Mom and me two small cups of soup called Mannish Water, a "wedding delicacy." My cup had something unidentifiable sticking up out of the liquid. Mom wouldn't drink hers until after I did. So, acting all tough, I took a sip of what tasted like dirty dish water. Everyone around laughed at the awful expression on my face. I handed it right back to Dan and said "What is that stuff?" With a wide grin, he explained that Mannish Water is a thick soup recipe that is considered a delicacy in Jamaica. It is made from parts of the goat that most humans consider inedible. He jokingly called it, "Goat's Head Soup. You have to be man enough to eat it!"

The man who eats everything must not look down on him who does not, and the man who does not eat everything must not condemn the man who does, for God has accepted him. Romans 14:3

A Prophecy Fulfilled

Mom and I were in West Palm Beach, Florida, praying with a few ladies who had scheduled us to perform that morning for their Christian women's group. We were all in a circle, holding hands praying, when the lady next to me placed her hand on my stomach and continued to pray. I was a little shocked, as no one had ever done that before, but I kept praying. At the end of prayer time, I politely thanked the woman for praying for me. I asked Mom if they did that to her, and she said no.

After the concert was over, another woman asked me, "Where is your little girl?" I explained that I was married, but that I didn't have any children, to which she replied, "Well, during your concert, I just kept seeing a little girl standing between you and your Mom."

Nine months later, I gave birth to a beautiful little girl, Torie Alyssa. Some people might say that it was just a coincidence, but our family knows that it was a prophecy fulfilled.

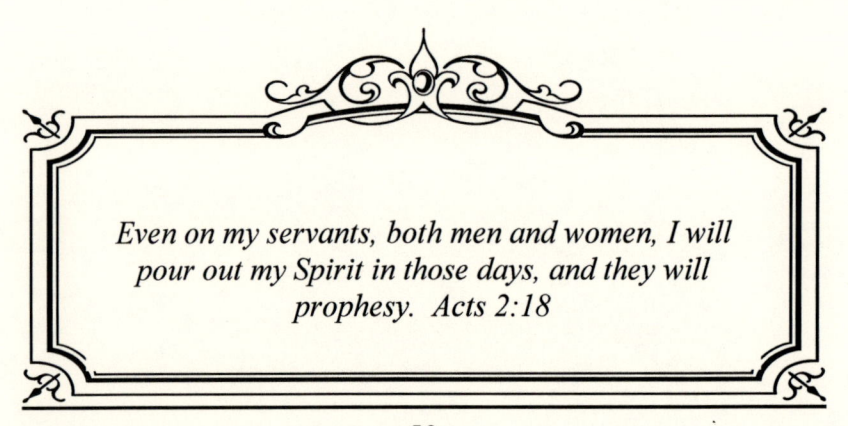

> *Even on my servants, both men and women, I will pour out my Spirit in those days, and they will prophesy. Acts 2:18*

Feast for Six

Sitting in a barbeque restaurant with our husbands and my brother, Rob, the waitress told us the special for the day. It was called, "Feast for Four." Since there was five of us, Mom asked the waitress if it came with enough food to feed five. She told us it would, and Mom ordered it. Just as the waitress turned to go, I stopped her and asked her if it would feed six. She smiled, a little confused by the question, and answered, "Maybe."

After the waitress left to put our order in, Mom asked, "Why did you ask if it feeds six? There are only five of us." John and I just smiled as I replied, "No, there are six of us to feed." Mom looked at Dad in confusion when Dad said, "Judy, I think our daughter is trying to tell us something." When Mom finally realized that I was going to have a baby, she screamed so loud the whole restaurant could hear her. Between laughter and tears, we ate a "Feast for Six" as we celebrated the coming of the first grandchild, Torie, and a welcomed addition to the ministry.

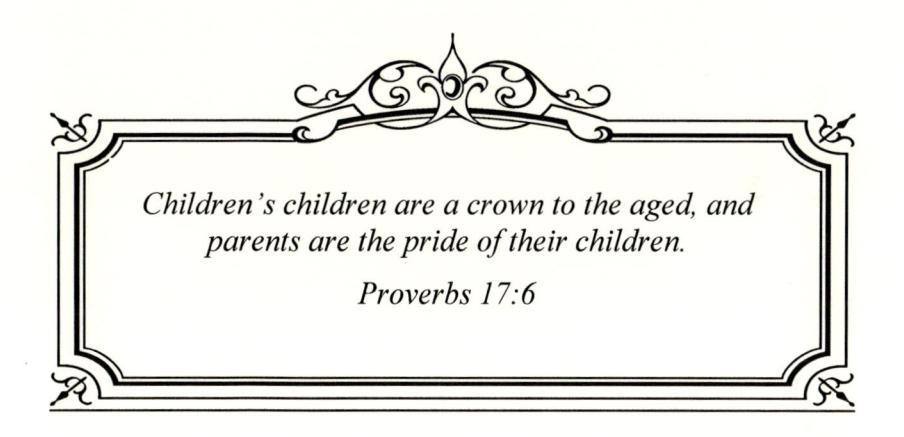

Children's children are a crown to the aged, and parents are the pride of their children.

Proverbs 17:6

A Gift from God

The time finally arrived for Torie to be born. Although there were a couple of complications, through the prayers of friends and family, Torie was born at 2:02 in the morning. She was healthy, and she weighed in at 7 pounds and 7 ounces. Upon arriving home, we soon discovered that Torie had very strong vocal chords, especially at 3:00 a.m. The problem was booking a concert at that hour!

The ministry van took on a new décor of bottles, formula, a stroller, and a package of diapers. When we asked Rob, my 17-year old brother, if he could help with the baby, including changing diapers, he said that wouldn't be a problem. Then he noticed the packaging claimed to "hold up to 12 pounds." We quickly reassured him that "that" was not what it meant!

We were all very grateful for this little gift from God.

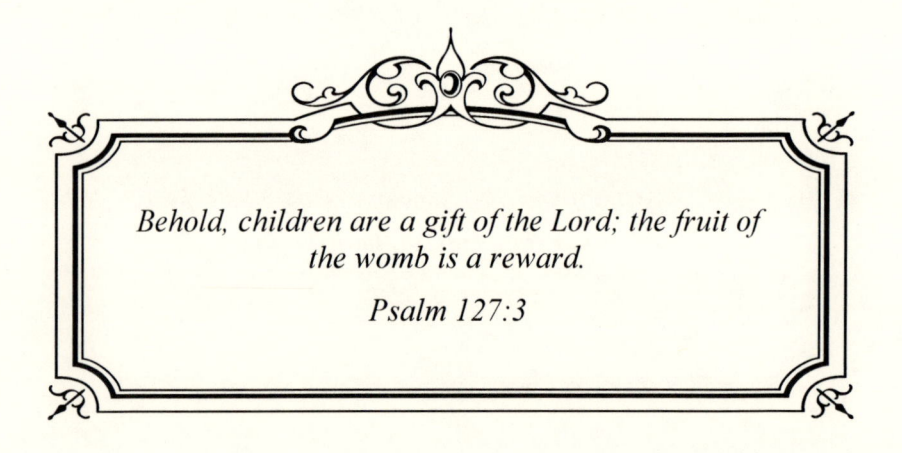

Behold, children are a gift of the Lord; the fruit of the womb is a reward.

Psalm 127:3

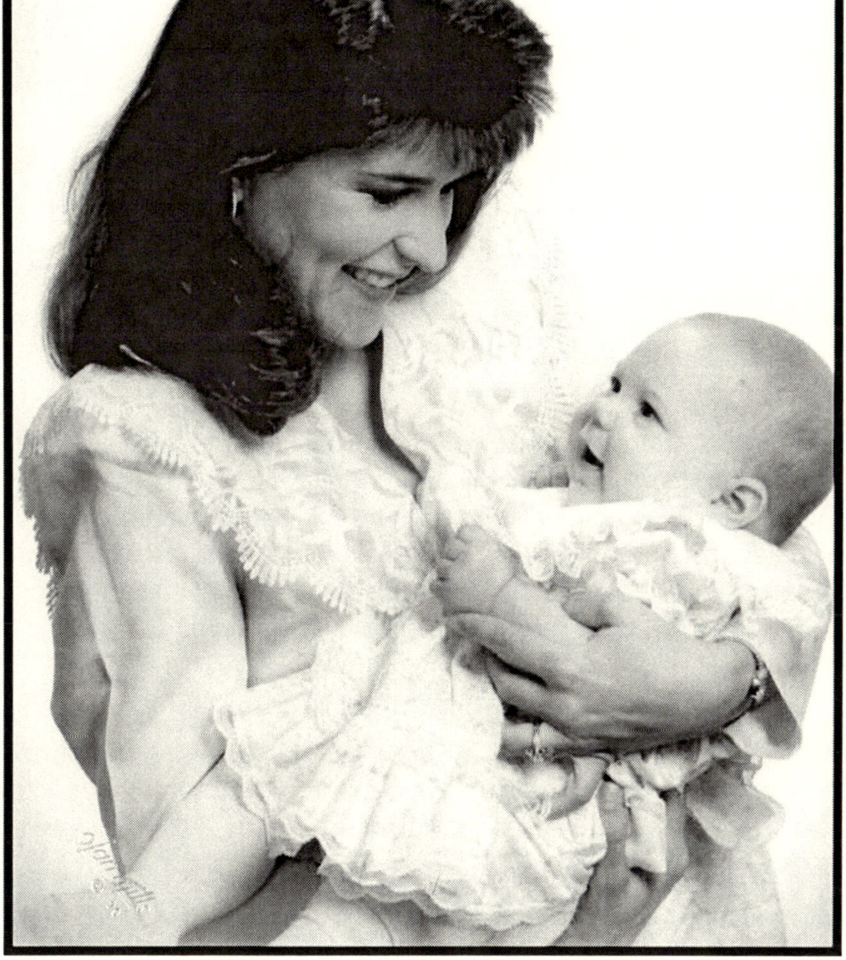

Empty Nest

I was married and already had Torie when my brother, Rob, graduated from high school. Mom was not prepared for how she was going to feel when he, her last child, went off to college. In some cases, we have heard other moms get excited and say, "Yeah!! Freedom!" or "I finally get my sewing and crafting room!" Mom was the complete opposite. An empty nest represented a great loss. Laughter and music would leave the home with Rob's departure.

Rob's pursuit of a music career took him to college at Belmont University in Nashville, Tennessee. The day Mom and Dad said goodbye to Rob at his dorm room, Mom barely made it to the car before she was crying. Throughout the thirteen-hour drive home, Mom kept saying, "The joy of the Lord is my strength."

After arriving home, Mom began walking down the hall to her bedroom. As she passed Rob's room, she paused, asked the Lord to protect her son, and closed the door to the now empty room. The door remained closed until my brother called to ask if he could bring a friend home during his first break. Mom and Dad were thrilled, of course. Rob ended up bringing several friends home for that visit, filling the house again with laughter and music.

Although it was difficult at first, eventually, the door to Rob's room was always left open. A few years later, Rob married Teresa, a beautiful, Godly young woman he met at college, and they eventually moved back to our home town.

Now, all the grandkids go straight to Rob's room when they visit Grandma and Da. Why? Mom turned it into a playroom just for them!

The joy of the Lord is your strength.

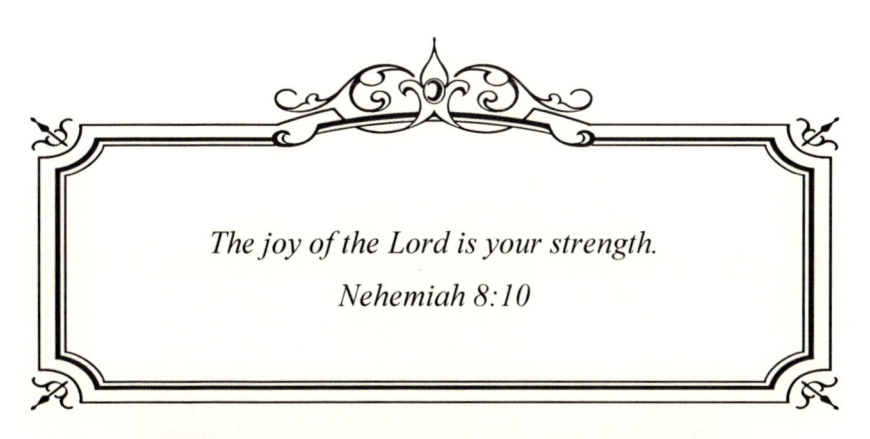

Nehemiah 8:10

We Will Carry On

Take Me Out To The Ballgame

When Torie was about three years old, she told us that she wanted to start singing solos. Since she had yet to record anything on our CD's, we agreed that it would be okay for Torie to just sing something a capella, like "Jesus Loves Me" or "Jesus Loves the Little Children of the World." That seemed to work very well until one Sunday, on the way to this little church, my Dad taught Torie a new song. It was entitled "Take Me Out to the Ballgame."

During the concert that morning, the time came for Torie to come up on stage and sing one of her favorite songs. She looked so cute in her little, frilly dress and her black, patent leather shoes. After Torie said hello to everybody, I asked her what song she was going to sing. She proudly announced, "I'm going to sing Take Me Out to the Ballgame!" In my shock, I quickly responded to her, "Torie, we're in church! Don't you want to sing about Jesus?"

"No, I want to sing 'Take Me Out to the Ballgame.'"

Finally, a kind gentleman from the back of this little church yelled out, "Let the kid sing it!" So, Torie sang "Take Me Out to the Ballgame." It was not spiritual, but everyone applauded when she finished.

By the time she was four, we recorded a CD entitled, "Young Country for Kids." This time, Torie recorded a solo that she could sing in our concerts. Of course, Dad could still teach Torie some new songs, but only on the way home from our concerts!

Sing to the Lord a new song, His praise in the assembly of His saints.

Psalm 149:1

The Perfect Family

People often see us in concert and say to us afterwards, "You are so blessed. You seem like the perfect family." Although we do feel very blessed to have each other, we are far from perfect. We have our moments of disagreements, like all families.

On one such occasion, we were to minister out of town in a church on a Sunday morning. At the time, our nanny, Jan, was traveling with us. Mom and Dad had already gone to get the van and trailer as Jan, Torie, and I came out of the hotel with our luggage. Immediately, we could tell that Dad was mad at Mom. He brought the van to an abrupt stop, and opened the trailer for our luggage. In his anger, he started rearranging the trailer, moving luggage and equipment with unnecessary force. Jan quietly, and quickly, I might add, took Torie to the van. I decided to stay and try to "help" the situation. I looked at Mom like "Why is he so angry?" We both knew that something had transpired between Mom and Dad.

Now, normally, if someone in our group was angry, the rest of us would try to minister to that person through love and prayer. On this occasion, however, I decided to try a new approach. I had the bright idea of displaying anger, too. So, I picked up the last piece of luggage, slung it into the trailer, and said in anger, "I can do that too!" Time, as I knew it, seemed to stand still. I had never spoken like that to my Dad before. In my pride, I thought, "Now, maybe he will calm down." Wrong! Instead, he slammed the trailer door shut, and we all got in the van without saying another word.

By this time, Torie was strapped safely in her car seat. As Dad put the van into drive and hit the gas pedal, we heard a loud thud. We were mortified when we realized that Jan had fallen to the floor of the van. In our anger, we failed to notice that Jan was still trying to get seated. She was fine, but we all felt horrible. We all apologized to her and to each other, but you could hear a pin drop at breakfast. Of course, we asked Jan to bless the food as the rest of us still felt unworthy.

Through repentance and forgiveness, we were still able to minister that morning in concert. No, we are not a perfect family, we just have a perfect God who loves us and forgives us because of His Son's sacrifice on the cross.

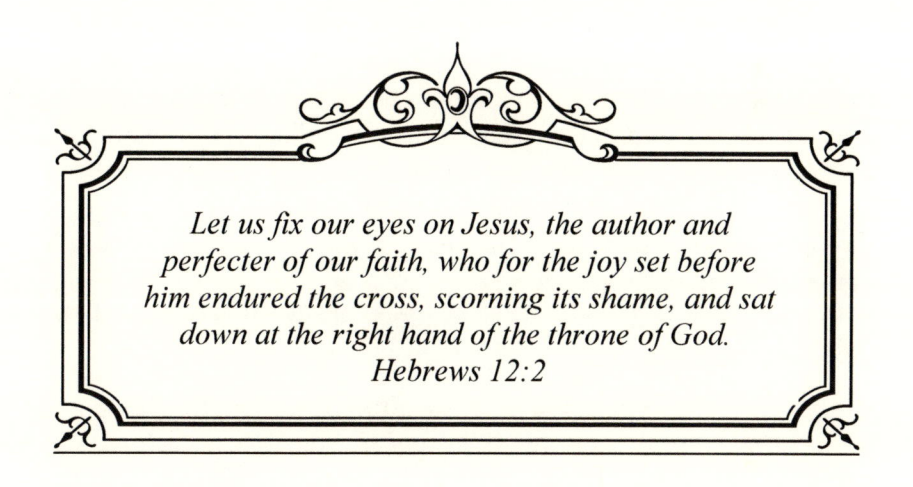

> *Let us fix our eyes on Jesus, the author and perfecter of our faith, who for the joy set before him endured the cross, scorning its shame, and sat down at the right hand of the throne of God.*
> *Hebrews 12:2*

A Common Bond

A mission trip to Mexico with a small child might be challenging, but not with Torie. She was used to traveling with us in the states, so this was just another "tour" for her. On this tour, however, we were traveling with several missionaries. Our purpose was to minster with a local pastor to his church and to distant villages outside of the city. Due to the size of the group, our missionary team had to be split up for one day. I was assigned to one group while Mom, Dad, Torie, and another missionary were assigned to go with the pastor. Later, we would all meet at another village where they planned to show a film of Jesus in an open square.

Mom and Dad's ride to the village was not an easy one. Most of the villages were at least 2 hours from the church. The roads were very bumpy and required speeds of only twenty to thirty miles per hour. The pastor drove a Volkswagen Beetle with a wooden bench for a back seat. The car was very noisy because it had no muffler and the fumes from the exhaust would come up through the floorboard. The pastor brought his 4 year old granddaughter with him so she could play with Torie. The only problem they had was Torie didn't speak Spanish and his granddaughter didn't speak English.

So, with the pastor and the missionary in the front seat, Mom, Dad, Torie and the little girl in the back seat, all the windows open on a very hot and sticky day, one hour seemed like forever. Torie and the little girl had only smiled at each other due to the language barrier. Finally, Mom asked Torie to sing Jesus Loves Me. She did, and then the pastor's granddaughter sang it in Spanish. The little Volkswagen ride took on new meaning as a friendship began. The girls were able to somehow communicate with each other for the rest of the day. They didn't speak the same language, but the Creator of music gave them a common bond.

All the believers were one in heart and mind.
Acts 4:32

We Will Carry On

End of the Road

After our Sunday morning concert, we all piled into to the van, ordered lunch through a fast food restaurant, and headed down the road to get to our next destination. We were touring in an area of the state that was very unfamiliar to us, but we had allotted enough time to get to the next church for the evening concert with two hours to spare. Mom had the map and the pastor's directions; I was driving. We were not too concerned as we drove down the four lane highway. It was after we turned onto the single lane road that we noticed the long stretch of road with no stores, gas stations, or houses, just wide, grassy fields. After driving for almost an hour, we were beginning to worry that we had taken a wrong turn. To make matters worse, the speed limit signs were slowing us down gradually with no stop lights in sight.

Suddenly, the road came to an end. We could not go any further as the road led right into a river, a beautiful, quiet river. No warning signs and no caution lights prepared us, just a large stop sign. Below the stop sign was a smaller sign that someone had marked through with black spray paint. Now we were concerned. We only had a few hours before our concert. Not only were we short on time, but we didn't know if we were even on the right road. As Mom and I analyzed the map, Dad pulled out his fishing rod that he hardly ever got to use and said, "Well, ladies, while you figure out where we're going, I'm going fishing! Let me know when you're ready to go."

It was not until we started to pray that another car pulled up behind us. The driver informed us that a ferry would be arriving in twenty minutes to take us across to the other side, and that it was only a few more minutes to the church. With relief, we sat by the river, watching Dad fish and Torie play. The end of the road wasn't really the end, just a time to stop and reflect on the goodness of God.

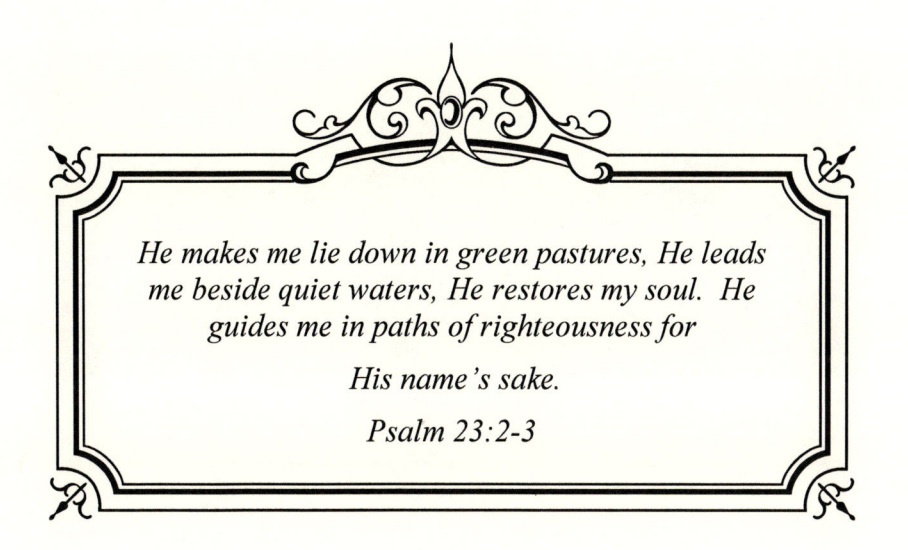

> *He makes me lie down in green pastures, He leads me beside quiet waters, He restores my soul. He guides me in paths of righteousness for*
>
> *His name's sake.*
>
> *Psalm 23:2-3*

We Will Carry On

End of the Road

Headed to the Races

One of our most interesting concert locations was at the NASCAR Race Track in Charlotte, North Carolina. We were invited to sing for the wives of the drivers. A luncheon had been prepared in a big, open tent. Singing over the loud engines of the cars preparing for the races was quite different from the quiet church buildings we were accustomed to performing in. Thankfully, we were provided with a large sound system.

Because all of the driver's wives were invited, there were both believers and unbelievers in the audience. We were very concerned as to how we would be received. However, as we shared our music and testimonies, and as women throughout the audience were wiping tears away, we knew that the presence of God was even in the middle of NASCAR.

Later that evening, we were asked to perform for all of the NASCAR families who wanted to come to a free concert. Our church building was a huge 18-wheeler that turned into a fifty-foot stage, and our congregation was a group of NASCAR families on lawn chairs and blankets.

So, the next time you head to the races, do not forget to invite Jesus. You might just meet someone there who would like to meet Him.

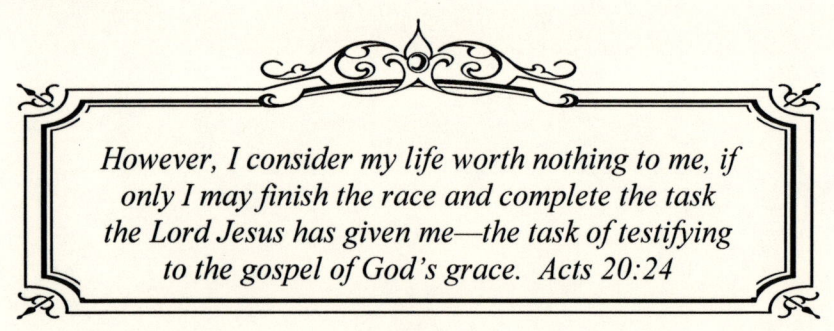

However, I consider my life worth nothing to me, if only I may finish the race and complete the task the Lord Jesus has given me—the task of testifying to the gospel of God's grace. Acts 20:24

Headed to the Races

We Will Carry On

"Many Rules" Motel

For the most part, hotel living is not a bad experience, and most churches are generous enough to house us in very acceptable hotels. However, there have been times when we have had to supply our own lodging between concerts, not knowing anything about the hotel itself.

On one such occasion, we were on a tour that included Florida, North Carolina, and Tennessee. Between North Carolina and Tennessee, we decided to take a route that looked like the best way to go. Hours of winding through mountains opened our eyes to the fact that the shortest path is not always the fastest. After twice the planned traveling time, we were exhausted and wanted to just find a hotel to spend the night. After two more hours of driving, we finally came to a small motel with a sign that said "vacancy." With no other choices in sight, we stopped for the night.

The motel manager acted very suspicious of us. Did we look that bad? He told us that if we lost the key to the room, there would be a five dollar charge. He proceeded to give us some other rules such as "keep the television volume down and turn out the lights when we leave." Although this seemed a little odd to us, we excused it and headed for our room.

Upon entering the room, we were startled to see printed notes everywhere on what to do and not do. "Do not use washcloth to remove makeup," and "Do not leave windows and door open when heater is turned on," and "Do not leave bathroom light on when not in use," and "Do not turn up volume to clock/radio." There were so many notes, and we were so tired, that we began to laugh. We laughed so loud that we thought at any minute he would come and ask us to leave.

The next morning, we were grateful for a peaceful night's rest, and we checked out, making sure we obeyed all the "check out" rules. We soon discovered that had we driven just a few more miles the night before, we would have come to a very nice town with several hotels and restaurants. So, we made up our own rule, "Do not stop driving until we come to familiar territory!"

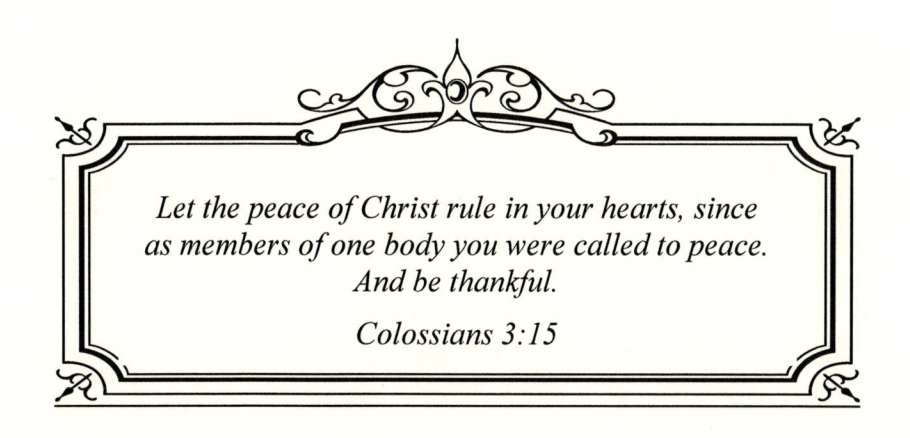

> *Let the peace of Christ rule in your hearts, since as members of one body you were called to peace. And be thankful.*
>
> *Colossians 3:15*

Walking on Water

Because our family has always loved fishing and boating, we decided to take a few days of vacation after a singing tour in the Florida Keys. Although John, my husband, rarely traveled on tour with us, he gladly took off work for a few days in the Keys. Dad brought his 17-foot boat, and after the tour, we were off for a day of fun in the sun.

We fished all afternoon, but we couldn't catch anything because two 4-foot Barracuda kept swimming around our boat and the area we were fishing. Anytime we caught something, one of the Barracuda would snatch our fish off the line before we could reel it in.

By early evening, just as the sun was going down, Daddy asked me to pull the anchor so we could head back to our hotel. The winds had picked up, and the water was rough. I was having difficulty pulling in the anchor. With the slap of one good wave, I lost my balance and fell over the side of the boat. Even though Barracuda are known to be docile fish, at that moment, all I could remember while I was falling into the water was their size and their teeth. Talk about Peter walking on water! I pulled myself back into that boat so quickly that I did not even get my hair wet!

We all had a good laugh afterwards, but my Dad traded that boat for another boat with bigger sides just so his "little girl" would never fall out again.

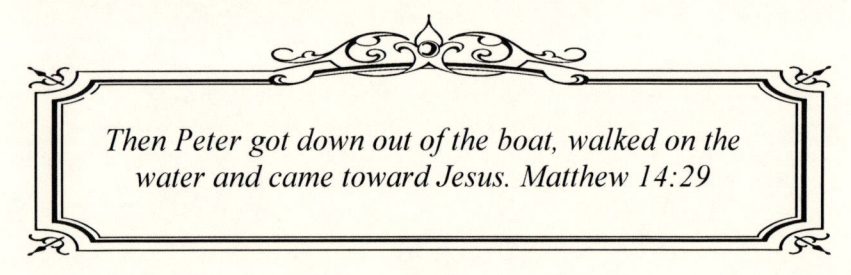

Then Peter got down out of the boat, walked on the water and came toward Jesus. Matthew 14:29

Smile Awhile

In 1993, we began producing a weekly radio program called, "Smile Awhile with Judy and Trena." The program was aired every Saturday morning on WAJL, a local Christian station. Our goal for the radio ministry was to start the listener's day with their focus being on the Lord and the joy that only He can provide. The program consisted of our personal experiences, humor, and a song or two from our recordings that went along with the topic of that day.

Developed from that radio program was a television special that aired several times on our local Christian TV station. This required several outfit and hair style changes to fit the segment we were recording. It was a lot of work, but a lot of fun, too. Mom and I are still amazed at the different opportunities God has given us over the years. I must admit that radio programming was my favorite. I could just wear jeans, a t-shirt, and tennis shoes, and no one would be the wiser!

Satisfy us in the morning with Your unfailing love, that we may sing for joy and be glad all our days.
Psalm 90:14

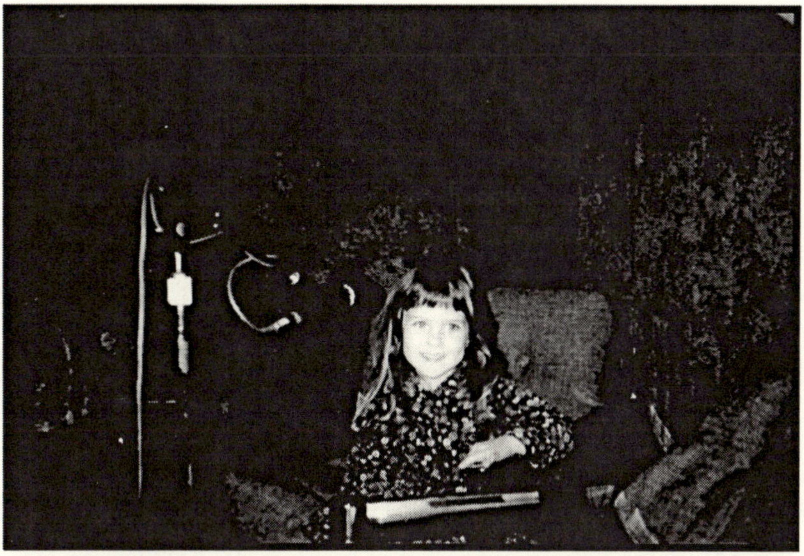

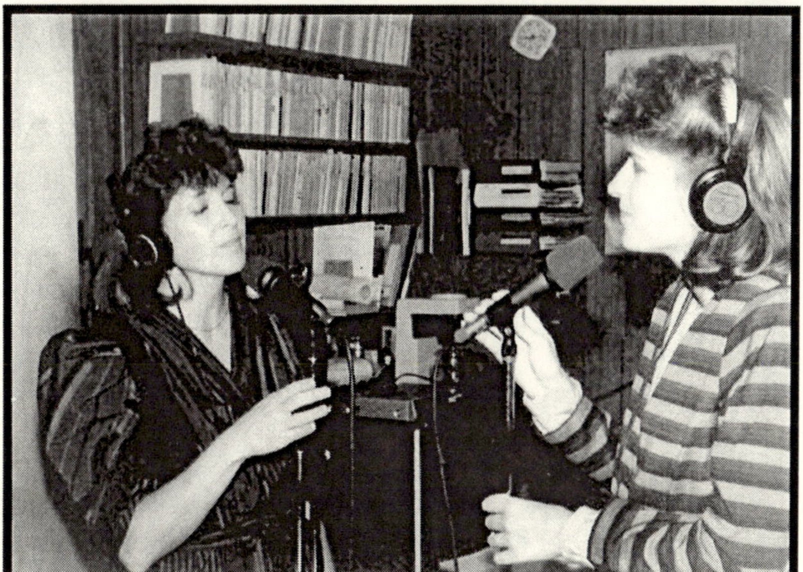

We Will Carry On

The Experience of a Lifetime

Words cannot express the life changing experience a person has when you go to Israel and visit the Holy Land. Just knowing that you are going to be in the same vicinity that Jesus was is exciting. Our family was not only getting to go, we were taking a group with us. At certain land marks, Mom and I would have the opportunity to sing a song.

The pastor that was co-hosting this trip with us had been to Israel many times before. He told us that because we were followers of Christ, when we stepped off the plane, we would feel like we were home. Being an American Citizen, this was hard to grasp. Strangely enough, as soon as we landed at the Tel Aviv airport, a feeling of being in our home land was overwhelming.

Each day of our trip was like going back into time and walking with Jesus. From riding in a boat on the Sea of Galilee to walking through the streets of Jerusalem, it was amazing to see firsthand the places we had read about in the Bible. Surprising to us was the bus station, near the Garden Tomb, where bus drivers still mock Jesus by holding down their loud horns while passing tour groups of Christians who are praying together.

Although every place we visited was special, the Jordan River stands out in our minds. Anyone in our group who had made a commitment to Christ at some point in their life was going to be given the opportunity to be baptized in the Jordan River. There was a place by the river where groups could come and rent robes for their baptism ceremonies. People from all over the world, representing many different denominations, came there to see the Jordan River where Jesus was baptized. Down by the river, hundreds of visitors were sitting by the river talking, while some stood and took pictures. It was actually quite noisy. However, with our CD player beside us, Mom and I began to perform for our group of fifty who had gathered together for the baptism. I sang a song called "Shekinah" while Mom interpreted with sign language. Before we even sang the first chorus, the crowds began to get quiet so they could hear what was going on. There were over 500 people there, but no one made a sound. As the song ended, everyone praised the Lord. I believe God placed our group strategically in the middle of all the other groups so that He could be glorified. Neither cultural nor denominational differences could keep us from worshipping together in the Holy Land. It was an experience of a lifetime!

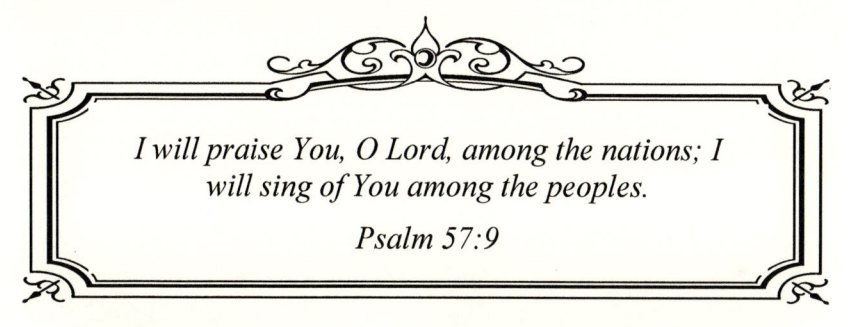

I will praise You, O Lord, among the nations; I will sing of You among the peoples.

Psalm 57:9

We Will Carry On

No Hands! No Hands!

While in Israel, everyone on our tour loved it when Torie sang about Zacheus underneath what is believed to be the sycamore tree. While touring the top of the rock fortress of Masada, many of us marveled at the view of the Judean mountains and the Dead Sea. Walking down Masada was exhilarating, but for some, the cable car would do just fine. Even the Dead Sea was fun as we watched a few in our group brave the extremely salty water so they could float without any floatation devices due to the sea's density.

However, it was the camel rides that had us laughing. It's not the camels that were funny, but the guides who owned the camels. Once we were settled on the camels, the guides would lead the camels by a leash and walk the camels in a large circle. Mom's guide was especially funny as he spoke very little English. Yet, he kept telling Mom the whole way, "No hands! No hands!" Now, for the professional camel rider, letting go of the saddle and throwing your hands up into the air is probably a cake walk (or should I say, camel walk). However, for Mom, just getting on the camel was a great accomplishment. We thought the guide would never let her down, nor did my mom, as she finally gave in, raised her arms in the air, and yelled, "Look! No hands! No hands!"

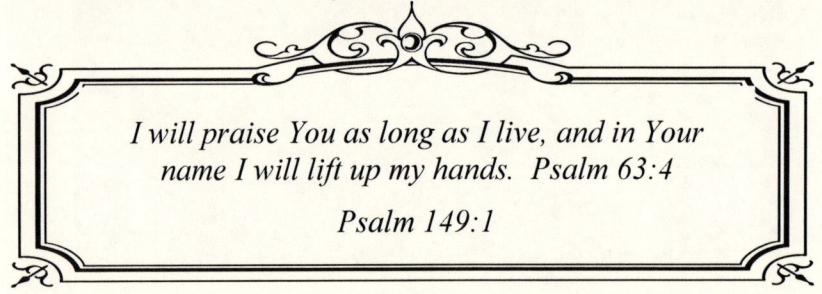

> *I will praise You as long as I live, and in Your name I will lift up my hands. Psalm 63:4*
>
> *Psalm 149:1*

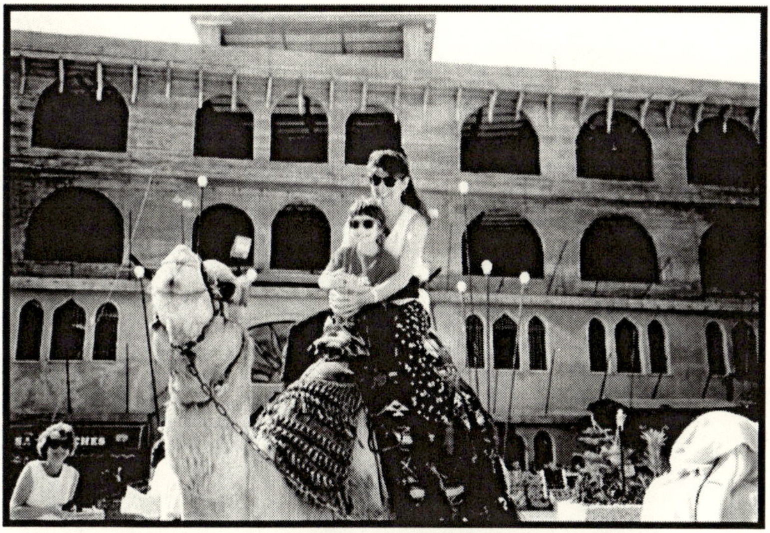

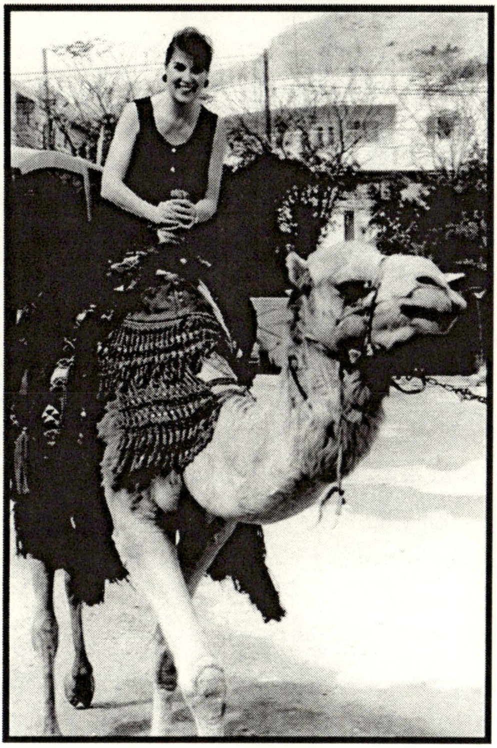

Dressing Room Dilemmas

You name it! We've probably been in it! Getting ready for a concert is always interesting, and sometimes, it's an adventure. Mom has always made sure we have at least an hour to get dressed and fix our hair and makeup. This usually leaves us plenty of time to pray before the concert, something we always like to do to prepare our "inward appearance" as well as our outward appearance. However, sometimes that is a challenge due to unforeseen circumstances, or should I say, dressing rooms.

Mom, Torie, and I have had the opportunity to change together in small, one person restrooms with one toilet. Some have had burned out light bulbs that make it difficult to put on makeup with any accuracy. Bathrooms in the South have had no air condition while some in the North have had no heat. We have not decided which we would rather have, beads of perspiration on our faces or blue lips. Most of those restrooms have at least been private, unlike the public ladies room at the fairgrounds where we had lots of people coming in and out, inconspicuously staring at us as we prepared for concert.

There have been a few occasions when we have sung at churches that have Bridal Suites. We were spoiled with full length mirrors and luxurious couches. However, most churches just have nice ladies restrooms that at least have mirrors. On occasion, when the ladies restroom was too small,

We have been offered the pastor's office (he was *not* in there) or the choir room (the choir was not in there, either). We have learned to pack mirrors and over the door hangers for our clothes just in case we need them.

When you are serving the Lord, you learn to be flexible. Our personal favorite was a broom closet. Need we say more?

I am not saying this because I am in need, for I have learned to be content whatever the circumstances. Philippians 4:11

Trials and Travelations (Part 1)

On rare occasions, we drive two vehicles to our concert destination. We were about an hour away from the church when a belt on our ministry van broke. Except for my Dad behind us in my car, there were no other vehicles in our path, allowing me to cruise safely to a stop on the side of a busy highway.

Mom, Dad, and I worked out the logistics of Dad staying back with the ministry van while the rest of us would continue to the church in my vehicle.

In eighteen years of ministry, we had never faced the trial of missing a singing engagement due to car trouble. God made sure that we would persevere through this trial by supplying a second vehicle.

In the middle of our concert, Dad walked into the sanctuary bringing loud applause from the congregation, praising God for his safe arrival.

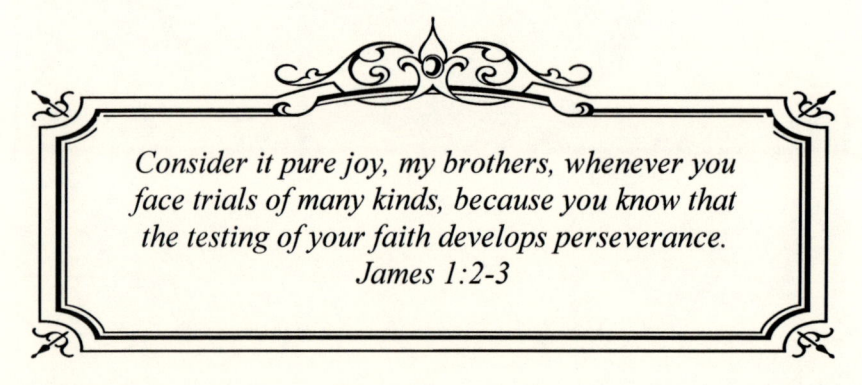

> *Consider it pure joy, my brothers, whenever you face trials of many kinds, because you know that the testing of your faith develops perseverance.*
> *James 1:2-3*

We Will Carry On

Trials and Travelations (Part 2)

After pulling off the busy highway, Ms. Jan, our nanny, took Torie and Jacob to sit on a blanket safely away from the traffic. For thirty minutes, Ms. Jan and the kids patiently waited while Mom, Dad, and I worked out the arrangements to get to the church.

After reloading the necessities into my vehicle, we glanced over at the kids, who were playing, and Ms. Jan, who looked a little forlorn. Right about that time, Torie came running over to us to announce that it was November 3rd, Ms. Jan's birthday. There she sat, on a hot, sticky afternoon, celebrating her birthday on the side of the highway, babysitting. To make matters worse, none of us had remembered. In the eleven years that Ms. Jan had sacrificed her time for our ministry, we had never forgotten her birthday. Today, however, we did not have a gift, and we had not even said, "Happy Birthday!" We had completely neglected to honor someone we loved so much.

How often do we, as Christians, forget to honor Jesus, Someone we claim to love so much? In the busyness of our everyday lives, we need to stop and celebrate His Sacrifice on the cross and His resurrection. Thank you, Jesus, and thank you, Ms. Jan, for your years of sacrifice to the ministry.

I thank my God every time I remember you.
Philippians 1:3

Spur-of-the-Moment

We try to book most of our concerts two to three months in advance, and certain times, like Christmas and vacations, are usually blocked off the calendar for family time only. So when a church called us the week before our vacation, and explained that the artist they had booked had to cancel just prior to their event, we had to prayerfully, but quickly, make a decision. Since we have always been careful to go where the Lord wants us to go (in addition it was on the way to our vacation destination), we agreed to sing for their "Youth Pastors' Seminar and Banquet." We just figured God had a reason for us to delay our vacation. He did.

A waitress that was serving that night stood in the back of the room and listened to our concert. We noticed she was crying when Mom shared her testimony about my drowning experience. After the concert, the waitress shared with us that she was not supposed to work that night, but was so glad they had called her in. Her little sister had recently drowned. We were able to minister to her, pray with her, and give her some literature to help her grow in Christ. We could go on and on about stories of how God has put us in places that we had not planned. We encourage you to always be ready to let God use you, even on the spur-of-the-moment.

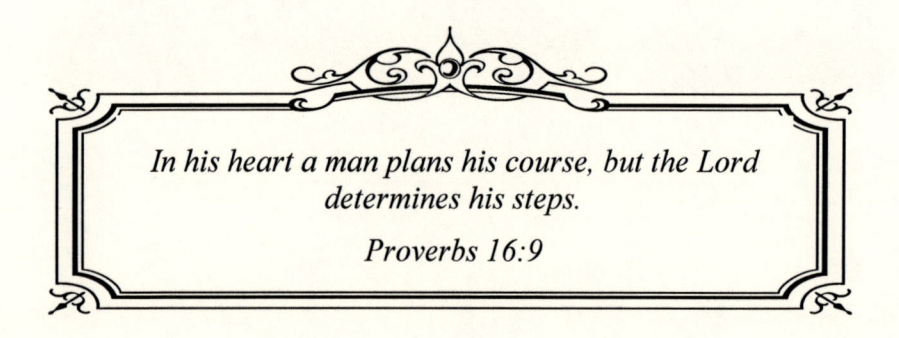

In his heart a man plans his course, but the Lord determines his steps.

Proverbs 16:9

Angel Dog

Jacob, my young son, always traveled with us. On one particular tour to Tennessee, we were going to be away from home for 10 days, and Jacob would have to leave behind his new puppy "Jasper," a Shetland Sheepdog. He was very disappointed, but Jacob did not complain about having to leave the dog at home. Well, God has a way of taking care of even our smallest desires.

The morning after we arrived to our destination, a blue-eyed "Sheltie" showed up at our cabin door. We could not believe it. Shelties are not a breed of dog that you normally see running loose, and we had never seen one with such blue eyes. He was so gentle and sweet. Jacob was delighted and asked to go out and play with him. The dog seemed to be just as happy to be with Jacob.

At night, when we returned from concerts, the dog was gone, but each morning, he would return to play. We named him Angel Dog. During our short stay, Angel Dog brought a lot of joy to Jacob, and it was obvious that Angel Dog loved playing with him. We never discovered who Angel Dog belonged to, but we do know Who sent him.

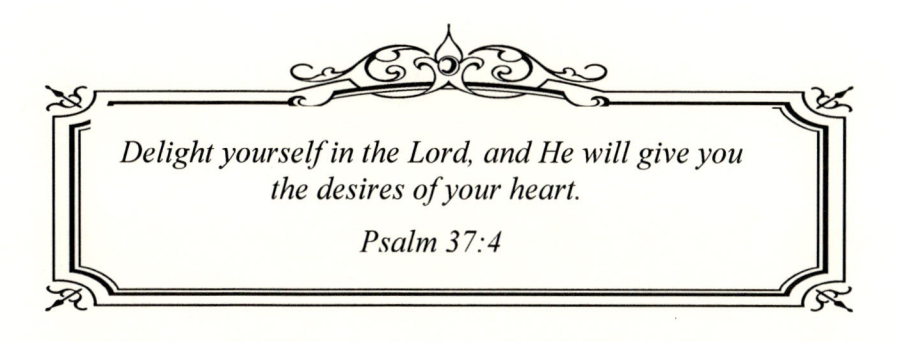

Delight yourself in the Lord, and He will give you the desires of your heart.

Psalm 37:4

Defining our Roles

When people have to work closely together like our family, it is important to define what each person's gifts are and how to best utilize those gifts. For example, Mom is very good at administration. So, she always manages our office and maintains the business end of our ministry. It is a time consuming job, and not one that I enjoy. Although I have helped her design our brochures, album covers, and website, Mom does all the paperwork. I prefer working on song writing, concert details, and ministry logistics such as setting up sound equipment and being the designated driver for long trips.

After many years of traveling, we have discovered that, prior to a concert, it is best if Mom and Torie set up the CD table while Dad and I set up the sound equipment. When I try to help with the table, I end up putting something in the wrong place. When Mom and Torie help with sound equipment, we all end up getting in each other's way. It just works out better if everyone has a responsibility and we all stay within those parameters.

As the body of Christ, we all have a role to play. God has called us to be members of one body, having different gifts, working together for the glory of God.

The body is a unit, though it is made up of many parts; and though all its parts are many, they form one body. So it is with Christ.

I Corinthians 12:12

We Will Carry On

People always ask us how much longer we are going to travel and sing together. The answer has always been the same. As long as God opens the doors of opportunities, we will continue to sing.

However, Mom began to notice that she was having some difficulty hearing out of her right ear. Before leaving for Nashville to work on our latest recording project, she went to an ear specialist. It was not until we had finished our recording project and we were on our way home from Nashville when the doctor called to tell Mom that the MRI had revealed a brain tumor. Specifically, it was a malignant acoustic tumor, and he recommended immediate surgery. As a result of the surgery, she would be completely deaf in her right ear, and there was a high risk of facial paralysis. This would end our singing ministry.

We immediately entered a time of prayer with friends and family as we sought answers from the Lord. Mom decided to get a second and a third opinion. The third doctor, a very well known and respected ear specialist, gave us a little more hope as he explained that the tumor was a very small, slow growing tumor and that it would be okay to wait another year to see if the tumor had grown any more. Although this brought some relief, we still kept praying.

We Will Carry On

    Mom started researching other alternatives to deal with this particular brain tumor. Through the internet, she discovered Cyber Knife, a fairly new radiation procedure that is noninvasive. Basically, the radiation slowly kills the tumor so that it will stop growing. To see if Mom was even a candidate for this surgery, she had to go to yet another doctor. He agreed that the tumor was still small enough to proceed with the treatment. After much prayer, Mom chose to have the Cyber Knife surgery.

    A year later, Mom went back to her ear specialist. Upon reading the new MRI, the doctor seemed perplexed. He was surprised to see that not only had the tumor not grown in size, but that it had actually shrunk. The Lord had answered our prayers!

    Although the doctor was surprised by Mom's healing, we were not. Long before we knew Mom even had a tumor, the Lord had given us the name of our newest recording project, "We Will Carry On."

> *Trust in the Lord with all your heart and do not lean on your own understanding. In all your ways, acknowledge Him and He will direct your path.*
> *Proverbs 3:5-6*

> *I, Jesus, have sent my angel to give you this testimony for the churches. I am the Root and the Offspring of David, and the bright Morning Star.*
> *Revelation 22:16*

Memories

First Album Cover "Friends"

Sharing a Comedy Routine for International Bible Seminary Graduation

We Will Carry On

Rob Writes Music for Judy and Trena – 1987

"You Just Can't Lose" - 1988

**"Young Country for Kids" – 1995
at the Beginning of the Photo Shoot**

**"Young Country for Kids" – 1995
at the End of the Photo Shoot**

We Will Carry On

Selected to Sing at Gospel Music Awards

Christmas 1996

Nobody Wants my Picture

Torie 8-Years Old

"You Show Me Love" - 1998

We Will Carry On

Rob Rogers, our Favorite Song Writer & Producer

Dad Making Traveling Fun

Trena's Son Jacob Joins us on Stage

We Will Carry On

Dad Always Teaching Jacob

Singing Background Vocals at Disney 2007

John, Trena, Torie & Jacob

Judy and Bob

We Will Carry On

Torie · Trena · John · Rob · Teresa · Emma
Jacob · Bob · Judy · Ellie

The Family

Christmas

Holiday Food

We Will Carry On

Holiday Food
Words and music by Trena Rogers

I love everything there is about Christmas
Oh the tree with the tinsel shining bright
And the cards from our loved ones just warms my heart
Like a log on the fire on a cold December night
But to tell you the truth
 If I had to make a list of things that put me in the Christmas mood
No it wouldn't be the gifts that put a smile on my face
It is definitely holiday food.

I like Christmas turkey with the dressing on the side
Lots of gravy where my mashed potatoes hide
Green bean casserole with onions that are chopped
Sweet potatoes with the pecans on the top
Sweet creamy butter with rolls of every kind
Poppy seed and pumpernickel
White and wheat and rye
Cranberry sauce with grated orange peel
I'm getting so excited and it's only the first meal

Ham, steaks, chicken baked with vegetables galore
Carrots, squash, asparagus and peas and cream style corn
Broccoli almond casserole with rice and melted cheese
My first serving's so delicious that I ask for seconds please

When I've finished Christmas dinner
I can't imagine wanting more
Until I look across the room and see a table by the door
There's so much for me to choose from
That it's got me mesmerized
I take a clean desert plate for cookies, cakes, and pies

There's apple, pumpkin, pecan pie and homemade mincemeat too
Banana cream and cocoanut and butterscotcharoos

Chocolate covered cherries and some peanut butter balls
Grandma's fudge and brownies taste so good
But that's not all
Jelly rolls and cream puffs, sugar cookies that are baked
To look like Christmas ornaments sitting by a small fruit cake

Wait a minute; fruit cake? I don't like fruitcake!

I like almost everything about Christmas
Although fruit cake shouldn't be on my list
But I'm sure there is more of the food that I adore
So let's eat,
Bon appetite
Merry Christmas

© 2003 NBM Productions

God Is Great
(Giver of All Good Things)
Words and music by Rob Rogers

God is great; He's the giver of all good things
God is great; He's the giver of all good things
In my heart I know it's true
That's why I can sing
  Oh that God is great He's the giver of all good things

God is great; He's the giver of all good things
God is great; He's the giver of all good things
In my heart I know it's true
That's why I can sing
  Oh that God is great He's the giver of all good things

We're greatly blessed, fully forgiven
We're eternally loved and His grace is freely given
O God is great He's the giver of all good things

God is great; He's the giver of all good things
God is great; He's the giver of all good things
In my heart I know it's true
That's why I can sing
  Oh that God is great He's the giver of all good things

We're greatly blessed, fully forgiven
We're eternally loved and His grace is freely given
O God is great; He's the giver of all good things

God is great; God is good
God provides like He said He would

God You are great; God You are good
God You provide like You said You would

God You're great; You're the giver of all good things
God You're great; You're the giver of all good things
In my heart I know it's true
That's why I can sing
Oh that God You're great; You're the giver of all good things

Oh God You're great; You're the giver of all good things

© 2005 NBM Productions

We Will Carry On

We've Come To Worship You
Words and music by Rob Rogers

We've come to worship You
We've come to worship You
We've come to worship You, Oh God

We've come to seek Your face
We've come to seek Your face
We've come to seek Your face, Oh God

Gathered around Your throne
Lord will You make our heart's Your home
So we can worship You alone
You alone

Draw closer to us now
Draw closer to us now
Draw closer to us now
Oh God

Laying our burdens down
Setting our feet on holy ground
We want Your presence to be found
All around

© 2005 NBM Productions

Wonderful To Me

Words and music by Rob Rogers

This is my hallelujah love song
This is the way I feel for You
This is exactly what I need
When I worship You

This is coming from my spirit
This is everything that's true
This is my holy celebration
When I worship You

Hallelujah
I love You
I need You here with me, yeah
You are righteous and holy
My heart's one and only
You are wonderful to me
You are wonderful to me
Wonderful to me

© 2005 NBM Productions

You're the One Who is Holding My Heart

Words and music by Rob Rogers

You're the One who is holding my heart…

No one's ever loved me quite like You do
This love is eternal
No one's ever shown me
The grace that you do
Oh it's true
I won't declare by any means
I have You all figured out
But Lord I am convinced without a shadow of a doubt

You're the One who is holding my heart
You're the One who has loved me from the start
And where ever I go, I know, You'll never depart
Cause You're the One who is holding my heart

Nothing satisfies me like walking with You
And just being in Your presence
The joy that overcomes me
When I delight in You, yeah it's true
The day that I gave You my heart
I never will forget
And the life that You keep bringing me
I never will regret
Whatever might come my way
Day or night, night or day
Your love for me will always stay
You're the One who is holding my heart

© 2005 NBM Productions

In The Name of Jesus
Words and music by Rob Rogers

Every moment, is a moment to become like Jesus
To allow the Holy Spirit, free reign in our life
Every day, is a day to live like Jesus
So that all who see, will believe

For we know where our hope comes from
And we rejoice in the faith we've been given
For the Joy of the Lord gives us strength to carry on
So we will carry on

In the name of Jesus, (transform us all)
In the name of Jesus, (we surrender it all)
Whatever we say, whatever we do
May it bring glory to You
As we do it in the name of Jesus
In the name of Jesus

So we will carry on
So we will carry on
So we will carry on
So we will carry on

© 2005 NBM Productions

We Will Carry On

Closer To You
Words and music by Rob Rogers

It seems like this world is turning faster everyday
And all my time quickly fades away
In the busyness I find I'm lacking of peace of mind
So I'm searching now to find a better way

If it draws me closer to You
And brings Your holiness to my heart too
Whatever it takes I will do
If it draws me closer to You

As I'm wrestling with choices
Through the day and into night
There is what I want and what I know is right
So until eternity my prayer will always be
For the strength I need that leads me to Your light

If it drowns out my love for You Jesus
I don't need it
And if it takes my eyes off You Jesus
I don't want to see it
If it brings me life abundantly
Then I want to receive it
Whatever draws me closer to You

Welcome to the Family of God
Words and music by Rob Rogers

Welcome to the family
Everyone here is glad that you came
Did you know that angels rejoiced
When God opened the Book of Life
And wrote down your name
A family like no other
In Christ, we are all sisters and brothers

Welcome, welcome, welcome to the family of God
Welcome, welcome, welcome to the family of God

You're a new creation
Old things have passed away
So leave your guilt behind you
In Him, you are forgiven, so don't be ashamed
Now and forever
We have a bond that will keep us together

We have God's word so we can live and breathe it
The leading and comfort from the Holy Spirit
The power to overcome, Christ has given
And in our prayers, we know God listens
We have a friend in Jesus
And no friend compares to Jesus
We have to love our sisters and brothers
And it all comes down from our Heavenly Father

You will find no condemnation
No fear of separation
Just a holy liberation
All because Christ Jesus saved and redeemed us
And we can say

© 2005 NBM Productions

We Will Carry On

I Can Do All Things Through Jesus
Words and music by Rob Rogers

I can do all things through Jesus, who strengthens me
I can do all things through Jesus, who strengthens me

If there's a mountain, I'll climb it
If there's an ocean, I'll swim it
If there's a battle to conquer
I know I can win if You are in me

Where You lead me, I'll follow
In happiness or sorrow
Through it all I'll be praying
That Your will be done in me
As it is in heaven

Your power, Your might
Your love working in my life
Your power, Your might
Your love working in my life

© 2005 NBM Productions

A Living Sacrifice
Words and music by Rob Rogers

Jesus, You are the Holy One
Jesus, You laid down Your life
Jesus, oh You became for me
A living sacrifice

Jesus, You are the Holy One
Jesus, I lay down my life
Jesus, I want to be for You
A living sacrifice

And my voice will praise You
As my hands are raised towards You
Every part of me is an act of Surrender
And it's all because of You
And it's all because of You

© 2005 NBM Productions

We Will Carry On

Judy, Trena & Torie - 2003

What people are saying about Judy and Trena Rogers...

CHURCHES

It has been our joy to have Judy and Trena minister in our church on many occasions. Their testimony is clear, the Spirit of Christ through them is radiant, and they minister through song in a marvelous way.

>Jim Henry, Pastor Emeritus
>First Baptist Church
>Orlando, FL

To say that Judy and Trena Rogers with Torie are both professional and talented is an understatement and the least of their positive attributes. What we at Brandon Assembly appreciated most about them was their warm and friendly Christian attitude and demeanor, along with their flexibility and their ability to work within the parameters of the outdoor community event where we enjoyed the ministry. That's why we wanted to have them back for a Sunday service opportunity. The quality of their musical abilities is just the icing on the cake of their hearts for people.

>Larry Ambrose, Music Pastor
>Assembly of God

Descriptive words for Judy and Trena are sincere and heartwarming through music and testimony that penetrate the hardest heart or sin sick soul. Don't hesitate to tap into their joy and energy for the Lord.

>Patricia Johnson, Pastor
>First Presbyterian Church

GRADUATIONS

Our graduation ceremony at the Orange County Convention Center, with graduates and visitors from 29 states and 10 foreign countries, was one of our best ever. Its success (Joshua 1:8) is due in part to Judy and Trena's personal effort, energy, and expertise. We appreciate their testimony and ministry.

>Dr. Daniel J. Tyler, President
>International Bible Institute and Seminary

THEME PARKS

A fine job with record breaking attendance...Our guests expect quality entertainment and Judy and Trena didn't let them down. Dollywood's staff really enjoyed working with this mother and daughter team.

>Judy Ward
>Dollywood Theme Park
>Pigeon Forge, TN

BANQUETS

Thank you so much for the inspirational performances you gave to the Premier Health members of our nine Florida Hospital locations. Your holiday songs were beautifully sung and wonderfully choreographed. Many people approached me after your program to tell me how much they had enjoyed the show. You all have a very special talent in making people happy—your faith really shines brightly!

>Beverly Gurtis, Bonnie Knowles
>Program Coordinators
>Florida Hospital

TELEVISION

Their music was really great, and I enjoyed interviewing them on ACTION 60's. I had lots of positive comments from my Senior Adults after the program.

> Herman Bailey, Host
> Action 60's WCLF TV
> Clearwater, FL

I know many lives were touched and encouraged by their ministry. We are so thankful that they were able to share on the Nite Line Television Network.

> James H. Thompson, President
> WGGS TV 16
> Greenville, SC

For Contact information:

www.judyandtrenarogers.com

ACKNOWLEDGEMENTS

Torie, who through her third generational influence, keeps us current in fashion and in music so that we can continue to minister with greater impact.

Tim Kelly, Fine Portraiture, and his staff, Curtis, Velma, and Tim, for great photos that have given our projects a professional first impression.

Juan Garnica, our editor and PDF assistant, for his encouragement and prayers.

Jan Laursen, our friend, nanny, and seamstress, for her years of dedication to our ministry.

Teresa Rogers, for your assistance in the ministry office and your excellent proofreading skills.

Our home churches who have equipped us for ministry through the teaching of God's Word, music, and fellowship of other believers.

Most importantly, to our Lord Jesus Christ, who sacrificed His own life so that we might have salvation and the joy that allows all of us to "carry on."

LaVergne, TN USA
30 October 2009

162569LV00005B/2/P